The Alpha's Path

How To Be A Leader

In A World Full OF Followers.

By: Jeremy Hanson

Contents

1. **The Alpha's Path** — pg1
2. **What is an Alpha?** — pg 2-7
3. **An Alpha is Honorable** — pg 8-27

What is honor?

An Alpha lives with integrity.

An Alpha presents themselves with style.

Always be respectful.

Don't let others disrespect cause you to act dishonorably.

4. **An Alpha is Honest** — pg 28-45

Why being honest is important.

Honesty begins with you.

Being honest commands respect.

An Alpha is always honest with money.

How to be honest and feel good doing it.

5. **An Alpha Is Knowledgeable** — pg 46-71

Finish school.

You don't need a degree but you do need knowledge.

You can't motivate others if you can't motivate yourself.

Knowledge adds to credibility.

Knowledge is an investment toward future success.

Learn how to leave the rut.

Stay curious.

6. An Alpha is Accountable And Responsible pg 72-87

Accountability VS Responsibility

Take responsibility if you want to be trusted.

7. An Alpha is Charitable To Those In Need   pg 88-111

What is Charity?

Do you have a big heart or just good genetics?

How to make a positive difference in the world today.

The world needs good leaders.

A gift that is given freely.

8. An Alpha is a Leader, not a Boss   pg 112-144

What it really means to be a leader.

Do you really want to succeed?

How to be a leader and not just a boss.

Get more done by delegating.

How to lead your team without micromanaging.

Why leaders are so important.

How to be a leader in your life.

9. An Alpha is a Warrior and Will Not Run   pg 145-167

The only way to get through your day is to be a warrior.

How to deal with stress.

How to be more confident in yourself.

How to get a raise without any prior experience.

How to handle a difficult conversation/ confrontation.

Stop running away from the life you deserve.

10. An Alpha Can't Submit   pg 168-182

Why an Alpha can't submit.

The meaning of submission.

How I discovered my True Alpha nature.

11. An Alpha Embraces Their Own Humanity   pg 183-198

The importance of understanding your own humanity and why you need to embrace it.

What you need to know about mental health and the Alpha community.

Is there a role for compassion in leadership?

The forgotten Alpha.

12. An Alpha Perseveres   pg 199-212

What is perseverance?

Always finish what you start.

Never lose faith.

13. **Conclusion**   **pg 213-219**

Not everyone can be an Alpha but everyone needs one in their life.

The Alpha's Path

An alpha is honorable

An alpha speaks truth

An alpha shows merit through deed

not sooth

An alpha gives shelter

To others in need

An alpha protects

And is willing to bleed

An alpha stands strong

When others will run

Though an alpha feels fear

They won't quit til they've won

An alphas a leader

Not just someone that shouts

Because an alpha is someone

Who knows what struggles all about

To be an alphas not easy

And sometimes they may fall

But an alpha gets back up

An alpha stands tall

What is an Alpha?

Some Alphas are born with the innate ability to lead. Whether that's due to a spiritual path that has destined that person for greatness or a soul that has been forged in the fires of the universe through countless incarnations of struggle, no one knows for sure. Others are forged through the fire of struggle they experience in life, and when faced with the choice to lay down or stand up they choose to stand. A few others are told they're Alphas by family members and friends only to find their true worth in the world. Some would refer to this as toxic masculinity, setting someone up for a lifetime of failures and remorse due to never learning the tools to be a leader. These few don't really end up fulfilling the Alpha role, but due to certain circumstances, they act as if they are an Alpha even though they aren't. This is usually seen in the scenario of the boss that barks orders instead of getting their hands dirty right next to their employees. Being an Alpha is about having confidence, not an overgrown ego.

I can speak from experience when I say that being an Alpha is difficult at times. The responsibility, the weight on your shoulders to lead others, to make sure that you are always there for everyone. It can be stressful. It can also be humbling and exhilarating when those times come along.

Throughout my life, I have been thrust into the role of a leader or a counselor so many times, and my experiences have taught me more than I could possibly put into words. Being a leader or counselor to others isn't always easy. In fact, it's very difficult and some days you may not want to be an Alpha (I know there have been many of those days).

It takes inner strength and self-confidence to lead other people – to push them towards greatness while also encouraging and supporting them through their weaknesses. It means leading by example so others can see how you overcome the challenges in your life. It means working hard yourself so others will work harder knowing they'll be rewarded for it. It means being consistent with your actions towards others because humans are social creatures who thrive on consistency, and they will follow the example you set for them.

What does being an Alpha mean to me? Being an Alpha means that I am the one who is always accountable. I have been told in life that as an Alpha, every action that I take and every decision that I make has a far-reaching impact on others. When things are going well, it's because of my actions and decisions which made those things turn out well. When things aren't going so well, it's also my fault. That's why accountability is such a big part of being an Alpha – when you're accountable for everything you do, nothing gets left out or skipped over because someone else was responsible for it (even though they may not be). Being an Alpha means that you're responsible for your actions and decisions – many of which lead to success, while others lead to failure.

Always holding yourself accountable and being responsible for your actions can be lonely and it's going to make you ask the question, "Why can't I just be like everyone else?" Trust me, I've been there. It's hard to be an Alpha and having to hold yourself accountable for everything you do – especially when the things that you make happen aren't always favored by others. Some people walk through life with an I can do what I want, when I want mentality, holding no regard for the effect it will have on others around them. This doesn't work within the Alpha's path. Many people that you hope will improve and elevate themselves to a level that can keep them in your life, aren't up to the challenge and will eventually fade away leaving you to once again walk alone.

It is what it is and anyone who aspires to become a leader in their own life should understand this because it's not going to get any easier later on down the road. In fact, my experience has led me to believe that being a leader means taking responsibility for more tasks and challenges than those who aren't leaders. Being an Alpha means that no one gets a free ride through life – they either work hard or they don't receive their rewards (rewards can take many forms including friendship, love, affection, sex, respect, financial gain, and more).

I will say that it's worth all of the hard work because as an Alpha you get a chance to make things happen for yourself and others. As an Alpha, you get to see others' lives change from being on their way down to going up in life through your actions towards them. That is a feeling that no one else can give or experience except another Alpha. The type of high that comes with seeing someone go from struggling to succeeding is what makes it all worthwhile. And the best part is, becoming an Alpha isn't difficult if you have the right mindset and set goals for yourself – which I'll cover later in this book.

Thank you for reading and I do hope you gain value from the content that follows. With the philosophies and mindsets held within this book, you will be well on your way to being the best version of yourself that you can be.

An Alpha is Honorable

What is honor?

Honor is the quality of being deserving of respect, consideration, or reverence by honoring others around you with the same. It is a strong belief that someone receives universal admiration by being of service to humanity and one's own community. It is a feeling of pride knowing that through your own abilities or achievements you have helped others in ways that they could not help themselves at the time.

Alphas have honor because they are accountable for their actions and decisions which lead them to success or failure. At the same time, they never let those failures hold them back from believing that they can do better or that they are capable of achieving greatness in one way or another. They have honor by being true to their word and living up to their obligations with other people.

In doing so, the people around the Alpha know they can trust them because they stand true to their commitments and won't break promises for anyone – not even themselves.

An Alpha walks tall knowing that others will respect them without having to demand it through loud obnoxious words or actions. As an Alpha, you earn respect through your character and actions – not by criticizing others who aren't doing what you think they should be or trying to force upon them what you think they should believe.

An Alpha doesn't need a little black book of people's secrets that he/she holds on to use as blackmail at a later time – it's not how an Alpha maintains and keeps their honor amongst themselves and others. An Alpha earns the respect of others through being honorable in thought, word, and deed.

An Alpha lives with integrity.

Integrity is the quality of being honest and having strong moral principles. It means that people can trust you because they know you will do what you say or follow through with your commitments.

An Alpha has integrity because they are true to their word and their actions, which shows other people around them that they care about doing things the right way. When an Alpha does something, he/she does it for a reason – not just because it's easy or convenient. They believe in themselves enough to make tough decisions when needed and live up to those decisions no matter how difficult the situation may be at any given time.

An Alpha doesn't have to brag about himself/herself or tell others how great they are (or pretend like they are) – because their actions prove that they are honorable human beings. They don't let themselves get comfortable for very long with what they've already accomplished before moving on to the next set of goals for personal improvement or growth, in any given situation.

An Alpha challenges themselves because they know that if they accept a certain level of mediocrity now it will follow them around like a shadow forever – holding them back from achieving their full potential as a person and leader. An Alpha strives for greatness by constantly rising above what he/she believes is the limit; whether consciously or unconsciously, but always striving to rise above whatever obstacles may be put in his/her way.

An Alpha has the courage to stand up against oppression whenever needed and to advocate on behalf of people who are suffering; not because they have to, but because they want to. As an Alpha, you stand for what's right and fight against evil whenever possible. You don't fear doing the right thing or making a tough decision even when others may disagree with it or try to stop you from doing it.

An Alpha always chooses the hard road over

the easy one because they strive to make life better for those around them and for themselves by never taking the route that offers immediate gratification but makes things worse in the long run. An Alpha knows that while short-term gains may feel good at some point, long-term satisfaction is accomplished only through hard work and facing challenges head-on.

They have courage because they have fought against their own self-doubts and conquered them; knowing that if they can do it, then there's no reason why other people can't do the same.

An Alpha embodies a balance of compassion, confidence, determination, wisdom, strength, honesty, and integrity. The qualities they have within themselves make them worthy to lead others toward a better tomorrow.

They don't embody these qualities because they are seeking followers or admirers. They want to leave a legacy behind after their time on Earth is done so that others will be able to learn from what they did right or wrong throughout their lifetime; not only as a leader but as an individual human being.

An Alpha realigns themselves with their purpose every single day. It's their passion, and it keeps them going at all times. It's what gives meaning to their lives because they know there isn't anything else that they would rather be doing in the world than being an example for others (and themselves).

They don't live out their days as if they were already dead; living off of whatever achievements they've achieved and not striving for any more success or greatness in life than what they already have. An Alpha knows that stagnation is death – so they work hard to push themselves past their own limitations to achieve even greater things in the future.

An Alpha understands that no matter how much they accomplish today, there will always be someone waiting in the wings, with good or bad intentions, to take their place as the leader of a group or movement – so they never rest on their laurels and always seek new challenges to conquer.

They don't aspire to be a good leader – but an example for others who want to become great leaders themselves someday.

An Alpha presents themselves with style.

Your integrity also comes in the form of not looking like a slob when you enter a room. Though it may be a style all your own and one that isn't necessarily on point with the latest trends, it is a style nonetheless, and shows respect to others around you, telling them that you value their opinion of you. This is a sign of maturity and will command the respect of others. It's also part of your leadership style to set standards for yourself that can be an inspiration to others in their own lives.

An Alpha has integrity because they have no

need or desire to put on airs about who they are; whether as a leader, an individual person, or even just someone who shows up to work every single day trying their best. They're real instead of putting on a fake persona out of a desperate need to be liked rather than being respected. It's their way of being self-confident enough in themselves to know that no one is ever going to like them for the wrong reasons, so they don't care too much about what people think about them. In fact, they're more concerned with what other people are actually feeling than what they may say out loud; which makes it easier for them to trust and connect with others.

Your level of integrity is like a shield that protects you from an onslaught of criticism, doubt, negativity, or even worse – people using your own kindheartedness against you for their selfish gain. It's something that very few people see worth having in this world but the ones who do understand its importance. When your sole motive for doing things is the goodwill or positive impact on others rather than your own gain, then you have succeeded in living with integrity.

An Alpha doesn't apologize for who they are – because to do so is a form of surrendering their truth and ideals to another person's opinion or point-of-view. They would much rather stay true to themselves and take whatever consequences might arise from others' disapproval over living life being someone they aren't. An Alpha knows that if people don't like them as they genuinely are, then there's nothing wrong with just walking away from those people altogether; leaving them with no one else to rely on but themselves. After all, it's better to be alone on top of the world than being stuck on the bottom with a bunch of people who don't really care about you or your success.

An Alpha accepts that they can't be right all the time and will even admit it when they're wrong, but there are times when they are unable to admit in public that they were wrong – because at that point in time, admitting such a thing could mean far more than just being publicly humiliated for making a mistake; something greater is at stake here. Therefore, their integrity requires them to do what is necessary to preserve what's at risk rather than admit defeat by bowing down and saying "I'm sorry" over some minor occurrence. After all, would you want someone you respect to say sorry every step of the way? It doesn't instill much confidence in someone if they constantly apologize for every minor mistake. It does more service to others when they immediately seek the solution to a problem rather than someone's forgiveness for a minor inconvenience.

    A true Alpha doesn't need recognition from others to know that they're doing a good job. They don't need to be told how awesome they are or even given an award or trophy for their efforts because the reward comes from within. The reason being, when you do something with integrity rather than just for personal gain, then your own actions will speak for themselves and people's opinions of you become irrelevant; in fact, some will actually reach out to you simply because they want to learn from someone whose belief system is viewing life differently than theirs does.

Your style, therefore, is more than what you wear, it is how you carry yourself and the actions that cause others to be inspired enough to listen and follow you toward success. Everything you do either builds or destroys your integrity and the bottom line is that by having enough integrity to do what's right over what's easy you are living an Alphas path.

Always be respectful.

An Alpha always strives to be respectful of others even in those times where they don't deserve it. In fact, the lack of respect or consideration for others is one sign that someone lacks integrity. A man with integrity will at least act respectfully toward a woman even when he knows she doesn't deserve his kindness. Everyone deserves to be treated well regardless of how badly they might treat you in return.

An Alpha's respectfulness is something they hold on to dearly and it's because they understand how important it is to have people in your life who you can really count on; just like family members who don't need your money or gifts but are there for you anyway simply because they care about what happens to you. This type of bond makes an Alpha feel more secure knowing that there are some people they can always rely on regardless of what might happen.

An Alpha believes in having the right amount of confidence and arrogance at all times.

Confidence can be a great thing as long as you don't get so full of yourself that it turns into arrogance – which is very easy to do. Arrogance usually occurs whenever someone puts themselves above everyone else; meaning they aren't really confident, just overly proud and selfish. A true Alpha feels confident about who they are but is more concerned with making others better than trying to make other people feel inferior because this type of behavior never gets anyone anywhere except far from success.

An Alpha knows that sometimes being too arrogant might not only hurt their reputation but also their ability to make new friends quickly or even keep some old friends around for very long. Therefore, they have the right amount of confidence to help them get noticed but are also careful not to become arrogant because it's very easy to lose old friends and make new enemies by being prideful.

Respect for others also means not alienating them with an unwarranted high opinion of yourself. Sure, you should always have your head up high while looking out for those who are weaker than you but never at the expense of someone else's feelings. Remember, everyone in this world has value and that is especially true because as an Alpha it is your job to figure out how each person in your life can benefit the whole of the group or the job you are seeking to succeed at. Sometimes the best way to accomplish this is by asking yourself what that person could do for you even before they've got a chance to tell you what they want from you. This type of attitude will also help teach you how to make people feel important which gives them an incentive, not only to support or respect you but also work towards earning more of those emotions themselves.

Don't let others disrespect cause you to act dishonorably.

There's always going to be someone that is going to test your patience and challenge your good nature. Some will be threatened by you while others are just immature trouble makers. There is absolutely no reason to stoop to their level because that behavior is dangerous and will hurt you the most in the end. Instead, be smart enough to walk away or allow them to walk away when they've got some things to figure out for themselves first.

An Alpha never allows another person's poor behavior to change their own integrity or honor no matter how angry or upset they might get inside. They also don't allow other people's negative actions to make them win by being dishonorable either. It's a fine line but Alphas know how and when to walk away from that kind of situation without giving up who they are inside just so they can feel successful again, right away.

An Alpha knows how important it is to take pride in their work but also to be willing to admit when they are wrong or not doing the best job they could.

It's not fun to have your flaws exposed no matter

how good you think you might be at something that is why most people prefer putting on a show of being confident even if, deep down inside they aren't so sure about themselves. Then there are those who just refuse to ever see anything negative about their actions and personal performances because they feel that everything should go their way all the time. Yet, it's these same types of people who never learn a thing from being corrected by others or facing rejection because everyone knows the risk in failure is an essential part of success yet, still, they choose their pride over trying again in another way that will make them better.

An Alpha realizes that failure is just a stepping stone to success and will do whatever it takes to get there as long as they are learning something from their mistakes along the way. They don't need others telling them what works or doesn't work about themselves, their actions, and especially about their performance. All they need are opportunities to improve in spite of any fallacies they might be getting from people who have either lost all confidence in themselves or have never been able to find enough self-belief to be successful at anything no matter how long or hard they've tried.

An Alpha has the courage and strength to walk away when someone else is holding you back.

There comes a time when we all realize that some friendships aren't meant to last forever. Some people are just there for a season and others are meant to be around us for the long haul. Still, we've got to learn when it's time to end our relationship with someone because trying to force two friends back together after they've chosen different paths in life is a waste of time that could be better spent helping other relationships grow stronger instead.

An Alpha knows everything has its purpose, but some things just don't fit into ours anymore so they need to be moved out of the way or tossed out altogether. It's not fair to hold on too tightly or try and make something work if it's no longer working for you or them because sooner or later, you're going to run into a situation where your decisions affect their choices and vice versa which is never a good thing.

An Alpha knows how to stand up for themselves without sacrificing their integrity or someone else's in the process.

A true Alpha knows that your word isn't always going to be accepted over another person's because you were first and they noticed it after you spoke it out loud. That doesn't mean that they are right about everything just because they appear to have a louder voice, more money, or better connections, but sometimes Alphas need to remind others that not every opinion is a good one. No one wants to be the bad guy or girl, and no one really wants to be the one who always has to say "I told you so", but sometimes it comes down to knowing when competition is a good thing and when it's just someone else out for themselves even if others get hurt by their actions.

Know yourself, and know your group because nothing can delay your forward progression faster than the self-serving nature of someone you thought had your back. Alphas aren't afraid to stand up for what they believe in, even if it means going against the grain. They know failure is nothing more than feedback and a chance to improve upon themselves and their actions so when they find out that they're not doing something correctly, instead of giving someone else all the credit, they will take responsibility for their own choices because this gives them more opportunity to succeed later on down the road.

An Alpha realizes what matters most in life isn't controlling everything or having everyone do things your way, but understanding how you can help others accomplish their goals better. They don't take rejection personally because every time someone says "no" to you, it just means they're one step closer to someone that will say yes. You can't please everyone all the time, s move on and improve upon yourself until you get that yes.

Rejection, confrontation, and obstacles are all just tests and an opportunity to improve on ourselves so we perform better the next time.

An Alpha Is Honest

Why being honest is important

Our honesty is the foundation by which others judge whether or not they can trust us. He who is not honest in little things cannot be trusted in important ones. We all put on an act sometimes, to get a girl or make a sale, but an alpha knows that dishonesty will only hurt you in the long run. When you're honest you never have to remember the story because it was all true, to begin with. Do what comes naturally. Flash and embellishment may make the sale or get the girl but in the long run, the truth will save your reputation and keep people coming back for more. "Just the facts ma'am" is a good policy to adopt.

When honesty and transparency become deception and obfuscation, the opposite of honest isn't dishonest. It's ambiguous. Ambiguity is not being clear about what we want or what we mean.

Part of alpha communication is setting clear expectations for others with our actions—because actions always speak louder than words. If your date walks out of the bathroom and asks "did you like dinner?", an alpha can answer yes or no without hesitation. Unless your date cooked dinner. Then you might want to go a little easy on them; just a little.

One of the first lessons we are taught in life is to always tell the truth. Dishonesty in your actions costs you that which you value most; trust. When leaders mislead their teams they forget that all deception eventually catches up with them. When they lie they must cover their tracks, or if those tracks lead back to something important: someone else's career or reputation for instance—then the leader is no longer acting on behalf of the team but against it and its goals.

When we are honest we never have to worry that someone else will contradict us or reveal our lies later on. People can always assume what you say is true—at least at the moment—because your actions back it up.

Honesty begins with you.

Honesty must first and foremost start within. It's hard to be honest with those around us when we aren't even honest with ourselves. We must remind ourselves regularly that we are good, we deserve respect, and we deserve the success that we work so hard to achieve. Only then can we be honest with others.

When our words don't match our behavior, it's hard for others to take us seriously. Merely affirming to ourselves that we are good and deserve the best will not make people see it, so we must also match this affirmation with action. Adding value through our actions is actually a form of affirmation. When you do good things they will know who you are.

Everyone has their own Achilles heel; their own secret fears that what they do—or don't do—doesn't matter. The Alpha knows that self-confidence is the foundation upon which all else must rest. Confidence is most often gained by experience; learning from failure or success in life, but sometimes we need to be reminded by others, or learn for ourselves that what we do matters. The journey may not always be easy but if you follow your heart and do the right thing those who you respect will notice and affirm your efforts.

You are a leader, act like one.

The stronger our sense of self-confidence, the more honest we become with ourselves about where it is we want to go and why we are getting there. When others see they can trust us because they know where we're going, then they will naturally fall in step behind us on the road to greatness. A lot of leaders get themselves into trouble because they lie to themselves about how long it will take, or even if a journey exists at all—because they can't admit their destination isn't always going to be an easy one to get to.

When a leader is honest with him or herself it will show in their communication and the choices they make. When we refuse to be honest with ourselves we lose our way; if not on the journey, then at least in communicating with others about where it is we want to go.

The Alpha knows that having goals isn't enough when there's no real plan as to how those goals are going to be achieved. For people to trust your plans, you must first demonstrate your confidence by setting clear expectations of yourself—and measuring them against reality. Leaders who set fuzzy objectives and fail to take account of results can't expect others to place much value on their words or actions, either because they don't know what's expected of them, or because their leaders don't know what's expected of themselves.

Trust is the cornerstone of any relationship.

Whether you are a leader, an individual contributor, or have simply been placed in a position that carries with it some level of responsibility—people will always seek to understand your motives and predict your behavior. This isn't necessarily because they want to control you or manipulate you; it's just human nature... as natural as breathing for us all. If people can't trust your word, then they must find ways to control you or the actions they take on your behalf. And while those who work for others might be ok with being micro-managed by those above them, smart leaders know that there is no such thing as too much trust—and would never want to work for people who can't be trusted.

A leader that inspires trust will make their followers feel safe enough to take big risks, and the best leaders will even be willing to do this themselves. You inspire others by your example because they have faith in what you're trying to achieve; they know where you're going, they are confident in your leadership skills, and therefore they are willing to put themselves on the line as a result. While some believe that inspiring trust is all about how soft your words are or how often you apologize; nothing could be further from the truth… if you really want to earn someone's trust then show them with your actions!

Being honest earns respect.

You can't respect somebody that constantly lies to you or tries to manipulate you to get you to do what they want you to do, so why would you do it to somebody else. When we're straight with people about what it is we want and why—they will believe in our words, even if they disagree with them. An Alpha knows that he or she must be honest to gain trust and respect, and therefore doing so helps build confidence in their own abilities as well as the people around them—especially when there are tough decisions to make.

Decision-making doesn't come easy for most leaders because of a fear of being wrong, but being wrong is part of any journey worth taking... otherwise it wouldn't be much of an adventure. Living life without ever failing at anything or putting yourself out there isn't living at all; it's just plain boring! When you live your life by always choosing the safest path possible you may never get to where you're trying to go. If you get there at all, you'll arrive with your best years already in the rear-view mirror. For some, this will be fine, but for those who are true leaders it is never going to cut it... because greatness comes from pushing ourselves beyond the places we've been before—and finding joy in conquering our fears along the way.

When I was a child my Mother would often share one of her favorite "Mark Twain" quotes with me: " You will be more disappointed by the things you didn't do than by the things you did." This saying has stuck with me throughout my life and taught me a priceless lesson: to be successful in life I have to take chances. If not—then I'll be disappointed by my life because it will have been an ordinary one. But if that's all there is for me… then I'm destined to fail spectacularly at achieving my goals and dreams! Failure isn't part of the equation unless you choose it; but don't fool yourself into thinking you can control everything or always get what you want in life—because if your objectives are set too low, then they're also too easy… "and easy never changed anybody's world."

As humans we sometimes live in fear of things that might not even exist, so why would anyone feel safe being their true self under the watchful eye of someone who they don't trust? The most dangerous thing you can do in any relationship is to lie to your partner. If they find out the truth and you've been hiding it from them… then things are likely going to fall apart because whether you realize it or not, seeds of mistrust will have already been planted between you both; otherwise, nothing would have ever been hidden in the first place. Once this happens, the foundation holding your partnership together will begin to slip and shift until eventually there's too much damage done for either one of you to keep trying.

The same holds in every facet of life. Whether the relationship is a romantic one or a professional one, honesty commands respect because it tells the other person that they can trust you. More importantly, it tells people that you value them and understand what they need from you. The more that people feel like a leader gets what makes them tick—the more that they'll respect their leadership abilities. It all comes down to personal relationships. To lead people you have to know them. Honest communication is the foundation of every relationship, so if you're lying to someone... then your ability to connect with them will be compromised from the very beginning—even if they can't see it! It is almost impossible for a human being to not trust another person who has been honest about why he or she does what they do and why they need their help because then there's nothing else going on but honesty. What more could anyone really ask for?

An Alpha is always honest with money.

One of the most important places to stay honest is in business; especially when it comes to money. There is always a paper trail somewhere that will show proof if you're not being honest in your business dealings. Fraud will ruin your reputation and most likely end up in a lengthy prison sentence. However, business aside, dishonesty with money can destroy friendships and end relationships.

Money represents power and freedom. It is a prize that every person wants but not everyone seeks to earn honestly. Some people will lie, cheat, and steal just so they don't have to work for what they want in life. Be wary of such people because while they may appear attractive at first—they won't remain so when the truth about their lifestyle comes to light. The one thing I've learned about honesty is that it's the best policy for every situation in life, because at the end of your days; what else will you have but your integrity?

    Occasionally, someone might feel like they can take an ethical shortcut by bending the rules a bit if it means that they can relax and enjoy their time away from work, but that's them and there has to be a limit on just how much they'll allow themselves to bend those rules before they start feeling guilty about doing things dishonestly. If you're not honest with yourself about how far you're willing to go in order to "get ahead", then find out as soon as possible; because while oftentimes this is all fun and games at first it will soon come crashing down around you if you continue to pursue such a lifestyle.

This is why an Alpha must always be honest because what good is all of your hard work if it all falls apart in an instant on the heels of some shady deal you decided to set up. Not to mention, you think your friendships and relationships falling apart is bad; try 10 or more years in a federal penitentiary for fraud. You'll find out really quick how lonely life can be, and depending on the prison, you better hope the best inside can handle the competition.

How to stay honest and feel good doing it.

In a way, this one is really kind of a no-brainer because it comes down to self-accountability and creating a pattern of honesty so you do it without needing to think about it. You'll feel good about doing it because the people in your life will trust you and things will run smoother when no one is worried about the possible ulterior motives you may have.

Sure, some people might not be able to take the honesty, but who cares what they think. If they think that way then maybe it's time for them to re-evaluate their relationship with you. Any friend worth having will accept and embrace your honesty, as long as there are no hidden motives behind your actions (those they'll deal with later).

You will also be able to more effectively help the people in your life. If you're honest with them then they'll appreciate it and when things aren't going their way they can count on you to have their back. This is especially true in business dealings where a client or customer can walk away if they feel that there's something dishonest about what you're doing.

There are many different ways in which honesty can improve your situation; it all depends on what your personal goals and desires are, but just remember this: if you aren't honest about who you really are or what your intentions are starting out, then no amount of money will ever make up for the emptiness that comes from living an ultimately false lifestyle. So always come clean early before it's too late and the person you're dealing with can't be lied to anymore.

When your integrity comes into question you understand how important honesty is. That feeling you get in the pit of your stomach when someone no longer trusts you is one no one ever wants to feel. No matter how much it hurts others or makes them angry at you honesty is always the best policy. You are the only one that is responsible for the choices you make in life and if you made a bad choice then take ownership of it and deal with whatever consequences may come from that decision. Seeking validation from others about a poor choice doesn't show strong character, it will keep people away from you because they'll fear being around someone so weak-willed who looks to others for support in making bad decisions. When the important decisions come around they just won't ask you and that lack of trust feels horrible.

The same strength of character and conviction should also apply when those decisions need to be reversed; in fact, it's more important than when you were first being honest. A person who doesn't have a strong sense of character and values will often keep making the same mistakes over and over again because they're not mature enough to face their mistakes, even if it means doing things right going forward. You can't fix a mistake until you acknowledge that it exists, but also be quick to admit your weakness for why it happened. Don't make excuses or go on long-winded tirades about how other people are wrong for making others dislike you; just admit to yourself that you need to change something about your actions and get started immediately on doing so if your goal is to stay on track. An Alpha always keeps their word no matter what; if they've made a mistake then they fix it by any means necessary, and when they can't fix it then blame is placed on them for their inability to do so.

These types of experiences will help you grow as a person, not make you bitter toward others who may have been the ones calling out your faults. You are responsible for yourself and what happens to people around you as a result of your actions (or lack thereof). If they lose respect for you because of something that wasn't done right in the first place then how can you ever expect them to accept anything else from the same source?

Loss of trust, respect and someone's desire to be around you because of your actions and lies is a feeling that will haunt you. Honesty is not only the best policy to have in life, it is one that will keep the weight off your soul when you look back on how you got where you are. An Alpha always does things with integrity; if you don't have the strength of character necessary to handle yourself properly then no amount of money or material possessions will ever make up for it. When you find someone who is honest with you then treasure them and their honesty because they are the types of people that are worth being around, no matter what decisions they may have made in the past. It's always better to be honest with yourself, even if it hurts than to live a lie by looking outside of yourself for validation on your actions or mistakes. Self-awareness will leave you free from those burdensome chains that hold everyone else back from achieving greatness; don't ever let anyone take that away from you.

An Alpha Is Knowledgeable

Finish school.

Knowledge is power.

An Alpha knows what they want in life and they will move mountains to get it. They won't settle for the things other people settle for, because they have internal motivation, a dream, and burning passion within themselves to become better than most people in their field. Someone with this fire within them will be successful, no matter what they choose to do with their life.

An Alpha is observant and always seeking new knowledge. They will ask questions so they can learn more about you and the things that interest you. An Alpha will make it a point to learn everything they can about these interests because it shows them who you are on a deeper level.

They know the value of knowledge and they know the value of a good education. At the very least, finishing high school sets you on the right track to success. It's not a necessity of course because there have been a rare few that have gone on to greatness without doing so, but it can only benefit you if you do.

An Alpha will never settle in life. They will always seek knowledge and they will never stop learning. Nothing is impossible because where there is a will, there is a way.

Dedicate yourself to your passions, dreams, and goals; let nothing stand in your way of achieving them...especially yourself. No one wants to be surrounded by those that speak without knowing what they are talking about, so know your stuff! Don't skip steps along the way if you can help it, and a good education is an essential step.

You don't need a degree but you do need knowledge.

No one is saying that you need to finish years

of college and get a degree to go on to greatness. I myself never went to college and have done fine for myself. I have been the lead singer in several bands, created songs with musicians around the world, published books on a variety of topics, and I am also a business owner. I did all of this with the knowledge I attained on my own and with the lessons passed down through my family. Knowledge comes in many forms, so don't assume that the path society lays out for you is the only way.

    The greatest lessons that I have ever learned in life have come not from books, but real-life experiences. I learned what it was like to be a leader when I was the head of a security team at one of the toughest bars in Portland, OR, and it led me to become a stronger person every day. The times when you feel inadequate and frustrated are the moments when you grow the most because they force you to learn about yourself and strengthen your weaknesses. An Alpha is willing to face their fears and conquer them head-on because they understand that only then will they begin living their dream life full of passion, adventure, and plenty of rewards for doing what they love!

Take risks...experience new things...learn as much as you can so that you can grow and become the best version of yourself.

Don't make school your prison. It's supposed to be a place that you go and get out into the real world equipped with the skills necessary to succeed in it, but more than ever school is being used as a source of income for those that are stuck teaching children to memorize information that they will forget before they even sit behind their desk for their first day on the job. I'm not saying that there isn't value in this because knowledge is power; however, when you have teachers covering material that no one will ever use later in life, which makes up a vast majority of what high schools teach nowadays, then we have a problem.

You may not need to learn how to diagram sentences and you may not need to know how to conjugate verbs, but is it really a waste of time if you want to be an amazing writer someday? I sure as hell don't think so. In fact, I believe that the best thing for all students in school would be to have a choice about what they learn. Let them decide what their life's passion will be and teach them everything there is to know but let them choose which road they wish to take on the way...if at all!

It is okay to skip steps along the way but avoid it if at all possible. Some steps may have been made up by someone that didn't realize they were a waste of time, but be sure of that because the steps you skip today may be the ones you have to go back and repeat tomorrow.

An Alpha understands that if they want something bad enough then there isn't anything holding them back from achieving it because there are no limits except those we place upon ourselves.

I have met many people that want to be singers, writers, actors, or musicians but their parents forced them to go to school even though those are the careers they would have loved. Parents think they know what is best for you and in this case, I would say that it isn't true. Don't let your dreams die before they ever had a chance because someone else chose what was right for you...they will never know your dreams better than you do so don't give up on yourself!

I am not saying drop out of high school if that's where you are at now because education is one of the most valuable assets to your future! If you're already past that point then do the research and see if going back to school makes sense for your life because there may be a better route for you.

Have a plan, work it, and make sure it's the one that excites you.

Don't get caught up in the trap of going down

a path that society has laid out for you because they are just guidelines...they aren't set-in-stone laws where if you break them there is hell to pay! Be who you want to be because life is too short not to do what makes your heart sing every single day of it! The passion that drives people forward fueled by their dreams will always beat strong over those that live their lives simply trying to survive each day.

The Alpha knows nothing can stop them when their mind is made up about something so why would anyone else even try?

You can't motivate others if you can't motivate yourself.

First and foremost you need to focus on your own motivations. You need to know the difference between a passion and a passing interest. You have to know what drives and makes you feel alive from one day to the next. The thing that motivates you every day and pushes you to be better. If you can't motivate yourself you have no hope of motivating others, so know yourself first and go from there.

Many people are motivated by having money. If they have enough to live a comfortable life they will be happy and work hard for that purpose only but if something else comes along that is more appealing then their motivation has changed! They need to focus on what motivates them every day because it's different from person to person.

There are Alphas out there with millions in the bank who haven't put two days of work into anything in years yet still manage to stay inspired, so I think you can find your own motivation without needing someone else to motivate you!

You also don't need others' approval as long as you can get up and go each morning doing what makes you truly happy. I know some people will try to tear you down for doing what makes you happy but ignore them and continue on your course. As long as you're not hurting anyone else or breaking the law then there is no other person that can tell you what to do!

So many people take pride in things they should be shamed for. I've seen people spend thousands of dollars on tattoos, piercings, vehicles, toys...things that end up being trash after a short time because society tells them "Hey this is okay! Look how cool we look!" They are sheep following the crowd instead of standing out from it. These same type of people spend more time with reality TV stars than they do learning about someone that's actually had an impact on their life.

We spend so much time being consumers rather than makers and we should be ashamed of ourselves for doing it! We look at others with jealousy, hate, contempt...whatever negative feeling you can think of because they have something we want but don't have the guts to go out and do whatever it takes to get it on our own. So instead of trying to make what you want to happen in your life, you decide that you're going to hate someone else for having it? That's sad!

The Alpha doesn't care about showing off or putting on a show. They just want to get the things done that need to be done...no extra flair or fluff needed! Once they know how to do something there is no reason for them to keep drilling themselves over and over again on a task that they have mastered. They then move onto the next thing and repeat the process all over again.

If you're not growing every day then you're dying!

You see this in nature all the time. A tree never stops growing or improving itself until one day it just dies. This is a metaphor for life if we let it be because the second we stop working to improve ourselves we will quickly become irrelevant in this world. The Alpha doesn't believe there is such a thing as being perfect so why try to achieve something which doesn't exist? Instead of waiting until everything about yourself is fixed and ready before moving forward with your life, learn to accept your flaws and continue doing what makes you happy.

The Alpha is not perfect and doesn't need to be. They are willing to work hard for their success and know that this life will never be easy but they also know the key to happiness is doing what makes you happy. So when others see them succeeding while they continue to hate themselves because of all of their flaws, they don't take it personally and they just keep doing what makes them happy.

We are our own worst enemy at times and it's time we stop letting that be the case. The Alpha knows this, and as a result, they learn from their mistakes, adjust their course accordingly, and go on to succeed because of it!

Knowledge adds to credibility.

The level of your intelligence and the amount of knowledge you have on any given subject greatly adds to your credibility in leadership scenarios or situations where you need to persuade someone to see things from your point of view.

The Alpha knows this and as a result, they pick up new skills to add to their arsenal. They don't just sit around waiting for someone to tell them what needs to be done or how something should be done. Instead, they get out there and figure it all out on their own so they know exactly what's going on before any of the other guys do.

There is no doubt that you'll look like a fool a few times stumbling while making your way through whatever project you're working on but that's okay because it shows others that not only are you willing to learn from your mistakes but also willing to work hard for success! Now instead of trying to come off as an expert, all of your knowledge is coming from experience which will always come off as more authentic than someone that's just trying to impress everyone with their theories and opinions.

Knowledge is power and if you want to be successful in this world, then you need a lot of it!

The Alpha leads by example which sets the tone for others. They are ones that everyone else follows because they know that if something bad happens, or there is a problem in one of the departments, these guys will get things done while everyone else sits around complaining about everything that has gone wrong! Everyone looks up to them as being leaders because they have proven time and time again that they don't back down from adversity before bouncing right back up stronger than before. They have studied the manuals, explored all the internet hacks, and found ways through their own experience to get things done efficiently and most times better than their peers.

This goes beyond not only wanting to know

how things work but also why they are structured the way they are. Once you have a better understanding of how things work, you can then manipulate them according to your purposes which is what sets great leaders apart from everyone else!

Knowledge builds confidence because it creates insecurities in others and gives you the upper hand. As a leader, don't wait for someone else to tell you where there is a problem or issue with something before getting out there yourself and finding ways through your own experience to fix it. Instead of wasting time analyzing and fighting over every little detail with another manager/supervisor, just figure out how best to deal with the situation by using your knowledge combined with your own experience! No one is going to know how you're feeling or what's going on inside your head so just take the initiative and go face it as best you can until the problem is resolved.

Continue to learn every day and stay

open-minded about everything that comes your way. With knowledge, you'll be able to get through anything that life throws at you without running out of ideas on how to deal with whatever situation arises in front of you. Time doesn't wait for us and there are always more challenges waiting for us, all we can do is learn faster than everyone else so we have a better chance of finding success before anyone else does.

To become successful, something I had mentioned earlier, build your confidence by using everything you have learned and gained throughout the years to rise above everyone else! Don't allow fear of failure to hold you back because it's the only way you're going to experience any kind of success. Question everything, do your research like crazy, and never stop trying until you figure out how best to deal with whatever situation happens in front of you.

Knowledge is an investment toward

future success.

Researching all of the latest trends and staying tuned in to the newest opportunities coming down the pipeline sets you ahead of the game. Especially when many of your competitors are busy patting themselves on the back for their last great accomplishment. An Alpha knows that pride comes before a fall, so they don't spend too much time celebrating success before planning for their next success. While others wait for one plan to fall apart before planning for the next, the Alpha already has notebooks full of ideas and investment opportunities. If you can embrace knowledge (whether from books, the internet, or your own personal experience), and then take action on it to make yourself successful, you're well on your way to being one of these A-list players in life.

When it comes to making money, make sure that it is not an end unto itself but rather a means toward an even greater purpose. Being rich/wealthy doesn't mean anything if you are constantly stressed out about paying the bills each month! For example, do you have enough money set aside for retirement? Do you know what type of car would give you the most satisfaction versus how much gas it's going to cost you? Or would investing in a home (or several homes) be better for your family situation than keeping all of your money invested in the stock market and waiting on that big break?

How do you want to be remembered when you're gone? If there is anything left over after taking care of yourself, your family, and any other people/animals who need support from you, then great! Use this money for causes that are closer to your heart. Supporting something like cancer research, wildlife preservation, or even something else that only you can decide on. Anything important enough to spend your time and energy on can make you feel good while creating a legacy for generations yet unborn.

Wisdom comes with experience, something the Alpha knows all about! When I said 'knowledge', I should have also used the word 'wisdom' instead because when it comes to financial success both are just as important! Wisdom comes from experience and an Alpha loves to experience anything that can enrich their lives and show them how to do things better in the future. While many (not all) A-list players have had an advantage over the masses because of their wealth, don't forget that they have had to work at it. They didn't just inherit millions of dollars and then sit back on their gold-plated throne ordering everyone around!

Flexibility is a must in business, so the Alpha has to learn how to roll with the punches and take things in stride when nothing seems to go right. If something doesn't go your way, figure out what went wrong and make some changes! Even if you don't care about making money, there are still plenty of other reasons why you should be investing your time and energy into improving yourself every day. The more knowledge you impart upon yourself, the better opinion everyone else will have of you! Because fundamentally, what people think about you directly affects what you can get out of life. Some people don't understand the idea of getting rich with little effort, but there is definitely a way to make that happen if you know what you're doing!

With all of your knowledge amassed and wisdom from experience earned, how will you use it?' There's no sense in putting this information to good use unless you put it to your advantage by taking action on it! You can have every bit of knowledge available (whether from school or through life experiences) and still not be successful without taking action upon that knowledge. In fact, a lot of valuable information has been lost throughout history only because certain individuals didn't think that they could put the information into practice themselves. If had they only known that success is a journey, not a destination!

So with your knowledge and acumen now in hand, what will you do?

Whatever it is that you choose to do with everything you've learned, just make sure that whatever it is... you're enjoying yourself. Because even though the world is full of people who want to take advantage of your willingness to share your wealth, there are also plenty more who just want to learn from someone else. Whether they have money or not! So use this new information how you see fit, then pass along some wisdom of your own if possible. In the end, we need one another for mutual survival so living life selfishly won't get us anywhere close to our true potential as individuals.

Learn how to leave the rut.

Don't get too stuck in your routine that you lose track of everything going on around you. Getting too comfortable can cause stagnation and make us miss out on a lot of opportunities that we otherwise would've taken advantage of had we just taken a moment to look around.

A new idea or experience is always exciting and your first instinct might be to say no. But, you never know how things will turn out for the better until you try! So treat every new opportunity as an experiment and learn from it. Remember that there is nothing wrong with making mistakes as long as you learn something in the process!

Also, remember that you don't have to do everything yourself even though many of us feel like if we do then we can't blame anyone else when it goes wrong. Plan accordingly and utilize others to their strengths; this Is part of being a leader.

As long as what you are doing has value it is worth putting some energy into. Whether it's for enjoyment or not, if it doesn't bring fulfillment then maybe it's time to move on?

You'll never know how you feel about

something unless you try it. All of the information in the world won't be able to save you from yourself if you just stay where you're comfortable and don't challenge yourself to do new things or widen your perspective! So get out there and see what's waiting for you to explore, even the simplest idea can have a profound effect on the rest of our lives. Learn how to appreciate every moment that life has thrown at you and leave your comfort zone right now!

Also, have you heard of the expression "You only live once"? That's true. And if we're going to be alive then it's important to make sure that every second is enjoyed and has some meaning behind it!

Being an alpha means being knowledgeable in many different areas. Being knowledgeable gives us confidence and makes us better leaders. The more leadership qualities that you develop, the more confident you will be with yourself and those around you will appreciate that as well. If you allow yourself to get stuck in a rut then you are not moving forward, learning, or improving and that's not being an Alpha.

Stay curious.

They say curiosity killed the cat but that only applies to people that don't stay informed to have a way out if things go south. The Alpha always has a contingency plan in case things don't go exactly as they envisioned. Curiosity coupled with knowledge is the key to innovation and it is your upper hand while other people are waiting around for the next great business idea because you're already creating it. We aren't waiting for an opportunity to come, we go after it. There are no limits in our minds and that's the way an Alpha operates!

Always research your options and see if you can make improvements before buying into something. You might not always be right but trying is better than never doing anything at all. Whatever you do decide; read everything about it, talk to people who have been involved with it or its related fields, look for hints on how things will turn out... etc. All of this information helps us build a history of what works best with certain ventures so we know what areas to avoid and what paths should be pursued further. So stay informed because knowledge will work to your benefit in the long run.

Also, remember that being an entrepreneur doesn't have to be all business. It's very important to understand how you feel about something before investing time and money into it. Do you see yourself enjoying the venture? Does it make you happy? These are great qualities that will help the future of your company in years to come because it wasn't just started for the sake of a job, but rather because it was used as a platform for your enjoyment and happiness! Keep things simple so that when opportunity knocks on your door you are ready with open arms.

Keep learning new things every day whether

it's from someone else or your own experiences! Knowledge is power and we want our goals to start manifesting themselves sooner than later! If there is one thing that alarms us most, is others thinking that they know everything. Because that is a sign of someone who hasn't been able to broaden their mindset and has stagnated in one place only to become lost in the many options life has to offer.

Knowledge will be our constant companion so let's keep learning about new subjects, people, or other things we can use in our future endeavors. It's important to ask questions and seek answers every day because it keeps us on our toes and helps us find new opportunities when they arise.

Life is too short not to enjoy it!

As Alphas, we should always make sure that we are enjoying what we do for a living, and staying curious keeps things fresh instead of boring or safe where we aren't learning, just surviving.

It's important to always be learning and

growing because knowledge will work for you in the future!

What does that mean?

If there are ways we can improve things, then let's do it. Knowledge is nothing without action and curiosity is just a seed of innovation. Stay curious so you can share your ideas with others throughout life! You never know what kind of opportunities will present themselves before they become reality. This will help us plan and keep doing our best at all times. An Alpha knows how to keep their options open when times get rough and everything seems hopeless. Curiosity can't kill the cat that plans ahead.

An Alpha Is Accountable And Responsible

Accountability VS Responsibility

Accountability comes in many forms and an Alpha at one time or another will experience all of them in their lifetime. It is how you handle each of these that will define your character and tell others whether or not they can trust you in the future. Accountability quite literally is being responsible for a person, place, or thing/project, and in the process of being accountable, you must be willing to take responsibility if anything were to go wrong. However, being responsible isn't the same as being accountable, let's define and examine these two words in more depth to understand how they are different and what their roles are.

When I was a child I remember my mother telling me that if I were responsible for something (like if she left it with me) then it would be up to me to take care of it; thus being responsible for it. Likewise, if I were to lose or break something that was left in my custody then I would be held accountable for the item because I had no one else to blame but myself.

So "responsibility" is a person's part in something and "accountability" is their responsibility towards others. If you are responsible for something then you must be accountable to others in some respect (or else no one will trust you to do that job again). For example, if I am responsible for making a sandwich for my daughter's lunch at school the next day but forgot to make it then I will have let her down. My accountability is diminished because I didn't fulfill my responsibility of making her a sandwich for the next day.

This second definition makes being accountable to others more clear and demonstrates that it is what comes after you have taken responsibility for something or someone, and that is why "responsibility" leads to "accountability". So if you are going to be responsible for anything/anyone then you must be accountable to a certain extent and you cannot let others down or fail in your responsibilities.

If you are willing to own up and take responsibility for something that goes wrong, then you are being "accountable". For example, if I am having a game night with my closest friends at my house and I forget to buy the snacks, then it would be my responsibility to purchase them and not let my friends down (and in this case, it's a good thing because they get cranky when they're hungry). Owning up to something also means that you must step up to whatever challenge is at hand and work through it.

An Alpha knows their responsibilities whether they have agreed to do them or not, so when a problem arises in their life they will know how to handle it (even if they don't have an answer right away) because of their own personal ownership over any situation which includes others depending on them for leadership. If an Alpha cannot take responsibility for themselves, is unwilling to take responsibility for mistakes that they may have made, or to be accountable to others in any way, then how can others ever trust them? A true Alpha must be honest and open about their character because a person that cannot recognize when they have made a mistake is also someone who won't admit it either. You simply cannot solve a problem if you are unwilling to admit to the situation and take responsibility for it.

An Alpha knows how important accountability is because, without it, they would never know what their strengths or weaknesses are or if there's something they could improve on. If someone isn't being held accountable in any way, then their mistakes will go unnoticed and unaddressed which will gradually lead them down a path of mediocrity (or worse). Accountability gives us room to grow; so don't be afraid to accept your accountability role when it comes to making a decision, owning up to an idea, or being held responsible for something or someone.

If you want people to trust in your abilities, then they must be accountable to you and others for their actions. An Alpha always acts responsibly and it's rare that they are ever truly unaware of what it means because they've already internalized the importance of taking responsibility for themselves and own up to any accountability that may arise from the situation. A true Alpha knows who they are, what their limitations are as well as their strengths and weaknesses; thus they know how far they can push things before their accountability begins (and they know when not to take on too much responsibility). They don't make excuses for themselves and they don't hesitate if they have done something wrong. They are confident in themselves and the decisions that they make because they know it's all part of becoming a mature adult.

A true Alpha constantly seeks out feedback from people because they want to be even more accountable than they already are and because there is always room for improvement (unless you're already perfect). An Alpha knows that having accountability makes them stronger, focused, works towards their growth as an individual, leads them to success, and allows them to succeed in any area of life or business. Being held accountable doesn't mean you can never make mistakes or fail; it means that when you do you aren't afraid to own up to your responsibilities, whether failure or success, so you can learn from them and improve your own abilities. Accountability gives the power to an Alpha to know that they have overcome a challenge or obstacle; it also pushes them to continue and strive towards what's next because they want accountability over their future successes. A true Alpha doesn't hide in the shadows of anxiety; they aren't afraid of being accountable for their actions because it leads them forward into whatever lies ahead.

Take responsibility if you want to be trusted.

I have run into too many people in my life that will never take responsibility for their actions and will fall on the sword of denial, blaming everyone else for their failures, before ever admitting their faults and moving on. These are people I can never trust again and because I once did give them the benefit of the doubt, it has caused me great pain in many circumstances. An Alpha knows that if they ever want to succeed, then they must take accountability for themselves and their actions, whether it's a simple mistake or something bigger.

Two instances, in particular, have shaped my view of the world and my understanding of accountability as well as responsibility. One was the time that got me sent to jail because I trusted a supervisor to tell me the truth instead of fulfilling his own vigilante vendetta.

I was doing security at a nightclub in downtown

Portland, OR. The night was pretty crazy and everything felt tense. It was one of those nights that I knew something was going to go wrong; I've always had a sixth sense about these things. A female friend of my supervisor was in the club that night with her boyfriend, a known drug addict, and gang member. As the night progressed he became very drunk and agitated, throwing up gang signs and being loud. The final straw was when I witnessed him pass off drugs to another patron. I approached them and informed them that it was time to leave. A request that he was not about to refuse, being that I am 6'2" and large. He wasn't happy about it but he wasn't stupid enough to test his luck.

His girlfriend was not very happy as she proceeded to argue with him the whole way toward the stairs. As they reached the top of the stairs he pushed her and as she tumbled down the stairs he followed. She sprang back up quite angry and lunged at him.

He pushed her through a glass dessert case. As I was helping her up while other guards kept him at bay he made his way for the door. Once she was up to her feet she pursued him again, throwing her cell phone at the back of his head. It connected and he stumbled forward giving her the opportunity to take him to the ground, mount him and begin beating him in the head. As funny as it was watching this small woman teach him a lesson, we still couldn't let it continue. We got her off of him which gave him the opportunity to get up and run. (Turns out she was a black belt in Jujitsu.)This was not my lesson, however.

We brought her back in the club for safety until we could be sure he was out of the area, but as the night progressed he began calling her from the payphone outside. After the tenth time, my supervisor informed me that he had spoken with the police and they wanted us to detain the boyfriend until they arrived. It wasn't completely out of the ordinary so when he told me and another guard to go bring him through a side door we complied. This man had never given me a reason not to trust him in the past.

As soon as we brought him inside I passed him off to my supervisor as another guard helped keep control of him. They brought him onto the elevator to take him to the security office on the third floor. All seemed normal until the door opened and the beating began. My supervisor started beating this man with what seemed like an intent to kill. The other guard who is still a close personal friend of mine went to jump in because he thought that was how we handled things, until I grabbed him, slamming up against the wall, and let him know that this is not how we did things. I told him to go downstairs and leave the rest to me.

After what felt like a UFC match between two equally matched opponents, (One where the other guy was using weapons because there was no other way he could win.) I disarmed my boss while breaking his wrist. My supervisor made his way down the back stairs as I got this walking piece of hamburger on the elevator. When I got him to the door I went to call him an ambulance but he knocked the phone out of my hand saying that he had a warrant as he ran out the door. Oh, and the cops had never been called.

The guy did end up going to the hospital with a cracked skull, the club fired us all but not before the owner laughed at me for taking sympathy on him, the cops arrested me as well as the other guard and my supervisor ran to vegas to escape punishment. I spent two months in jail before my lawyer was able to prove that the minimal involvement I had was only in preventing any further damage to the guy my supervisor attacked. Despite the help I provided in bringing my former supervisor to justice I still faced three years of probation and a hit to my mental health as I had to reevaluate the way I judged the people I trusted so I would never need to experience being punished for another person's mistakes again. (On a side note, the guy that got assaulted that night ended up going to the same jail right along with us, because this was not a good guy, folks.) Things aren't always black and white.

The second circumstance that taught me a life-altering lesson in responsibility and accountability was when my wife cheated on me with one of my best friends. She had always had issues with drinking, as well as uncontrollable violent outbursts. For some reason, I stayed through despite all logic telling me to get as far away from her as possible. Love, and yes it is love, makes you do irrational things.

What pushed things over the edge was when the cheating began. We were out one night with friends and someone suggested checking out the local swingers club. I was against the idea, more out of boredom with that scene than anything else.

Through my work in strip clubs and escorting people through very sex-positive environments as a bodyguard, I have learned that nudity, as well as sex, is just another drug that you eventually get bored with. If there is not an emotional connection behind it or a next level to push it to then you are frequently disappointed with the outcome.

My now ex-wife however started going to the club without me, sometimes accompanied by my friend, who I soon found out liked to push that next level by screwing other guy's wives. At least I wasn't the only one, right. He pushed a lot of levels though with drugs and drinking as well, so, no surprise I guess. The surprise is when my wife gave me the ultimatum that either she was allowed to continue cheating or our marriage was over...like that was actually a choice. After a lot of nonsense that I am purposely skipping over as to not make her look any worse than she already does, (ask me in private if you ever meet me) we got divorced.

Although my former friend deserves a beating the likes of which his grandkids will feel, I did not take vengeance and instead cut him off from everything and everybody connected to me that ever gave him support (which I guess is another form of vengeance and well deserved). I kept calm because I can't parent my daughter very well from behind bars. We make tough choices in this life for the ones we love but they are choices that benefit everyone, not just ourselves.

Yes, I do still love my ex-wife and will always be there for her in some capacity because an Alpha never abandons members of the pack; even the batshit crazy ones. This one also happens to be the mother of my daughter. While the mistake was not mine, (there is another lesson for you youngsters out there) I of course took full responsibility for my role in things and am currently working on my parental relationship with her as well as what can be salvaged from our friendship because that is what an Alpha does. It's not always easy, but you don't learn much from the easy choices in life.

If you want to be an Alpha then you have to accept the responsibility for all of your mistakes and take the responsibility onto yourself to fix a situation when no one else will. Remember that fairness does not mean equality except in math class. In life, it means if I mess up I had better clean up my own shit instead of expecting someone else to do it for me or I am not really worth much at all.

When someone shits on you, expect them to pick up their own feces but don't be surprised if they run away from this task as well...you get what you give in this universe. It's tough love right now, but someday I know my daughter will understand why we do these things, and then she can pass the knowledge onto her kids.

My child will be raised with both of her parents doing the best they can, with at least one (hopefully both...eventually) holding themselves accountable for their own actions and ensuring she is not exposed to any more violence or drugs than she has already seen. I'm still stressing about the sex talk but I have an open mind in that department so we can just go over it together when the time comes.

A pack that does not stick together falls apart. A pack without rules is lost. Pack first, everything else second. Now get out there and take some fucking responsibility!!!

An Alpha Is Charitable To Those In Need

What is charity?

Charity can be defined in a few different ways. The good-natured act of giving to those less fortunate than you, be it money or food or clothing. Or, it can be defined as a selfless concern for the welfare of others (Merriam-Webster Dictionary).

An Alpha gives even when they have nothing left to give. If an Alpha only has $1 in their pocket then they'll buy a homeless person something off the dollar menu because there weren't other options available to them. They might offer them shelter from the cold weather if they had it to give but wouldn't force anything on someone who didn't ask for help because an Alpha also respects someones right to live their life the way they choose. An Alpha isn't always rich by any means either, though that does not limit their capacity to help a person in need.

They don't have to say anything when they give someone something, because what they did was enough of an act of kindness without having to verbalize the gesture. Giving someone something without telling them about it is one of the greatest gifts you can offer someone in life. The only thing better is if you're able to tell them "I saw that you needed this, so I wanted to take a moment and give it to you". It's that act of compassion and love that truly drives your value as an individual higher than any amount of money ever could.

When I see someone on the street corner. I don't turn away and pretend they're not there. Even if I have nothing to give, the simple act of making them feel relevant and seen is enough to keep them going another day. If they ask for money, I'll hand them whatever I have on me at the time. If they want something to eat, I'll take them to a restaurant and buy their meal (most restaurants will let you do this). Or if it's cold outside and they're freezing and don't have a coat, I'll buy them one if I can afford it. A good Alpha can find warmth in any situation and share it with others.

A real Alpha doesn't hold back from helping someone in need because they think "I'm not rich enough or powerful enough to help them". They don't spend all day complaining about how poor/average/poorly-off they are. They'll either overcome their situation or at least try to.

Don't let the world tell you how much you can or cannot do. You are the master of your own fate, and can always find a way to help someone if you really want it bad enough. Sometimes this is accomplished by helping out local charities, giving them money when you're able, volunteering your time at shelters for those less fortunate than yourself (or just playing with/hanging out with disadvantaged youth who could use a good role model), and other times it's simply doing something as simple as smiling at a stranger on the street like they're an old friend, because, in reality, they might feel more alone right now than everyone else combined.

It doesn't matter what race, gender, or orientation you are in life. All that matters is that you help people when you can, and respect their right to live the way they choose even if they don't want anything to do with you.

The world would benefit a lot more if everyone just helped one another out (or at least tried). We already have all the resources we need as a species to be prosperous; we just try and find ways to hoard it and keep it for ourselves instead of giving back. It's unfortunate but true... sad but true.

An Alpha gives because they know what it feels like to really need help, to feel lost and alone without any friends or family reachable by phone call or e-mail. An Alpha gives because they want to be that helping hand for someone else in need. An Alpha gives because they know no one can do everything on their own, and if the only thing I can give right now is a handful of loose change, then I'll gladly do so.

Do you have a big heart or just good genetics?

Some help out their community because their nature from the day they were born was that of an amazing person with an amazing heart. Others do so because their parents or grandparents taught them to give back and it has stuck with them from childhood. Whatever the case may be, you don't have to be a certain way or be born into a specific family to be charitable and kind.

An Alpha doesn't always have the funds necessary to give away what they want, but that doesn't stop them from giving something small when they can. The bottom line is that some people are just naturally good people who believe in doing what's right no matter what their actions might cost them. These are the types of people you'll see on TV as heroes who save someone from drowning without thinking twice about it. They don't do it for personal glory, fame, or fortune... they do it because they simply wanted to help out another person in need who was close by.

There is no shame in needing money/help yourself either from time to time. We're all human and we've all been in a situation where we needed to swallow our pride and ask for help from someone we didn't know before. In the end, what matters most is that you regain your dignity by not being ashamed of who you are and asking for assistance when you feel it's necessary.

What matters is that you always strive to be the best version of yourself possible on any given day. One thing that some people tend to overlook though is how much better other people's lives can become because of one selfless act or random kindness shown towards them.

It's the one thing that helps to make a person realize that they're not alone in the world, and there is still some good left in humanity if you're willing to go out of your way to find it.

We've all been hurt at some point or another by someone we trusted with a lot of our heart, but how do you define yourself as a person? Do you let other people tell you who or what you should be, or do you become wiser from being hurt and make a vow from then on that no matter what anyone else thinks, you're going to stand up for yourself every time a situation arises? They don't know anything about your past nor how much time/effort went into making any decisions you may have made along the way so don't let other people's opinions dictate who you are or whether or not you show kindness from this point on.

How to make a positive difference in the world today.

With so much going on in the world, be it natural disasters, pandemics, crooked politicians, rioting, and just all-around shitty people; it's easy to start to lose hope. The thing is, you don't have to change the world to change the way one person or a few people view it. Through your kindness and generosity, you can help to make a real difference in the lives of those who are around you.

You don't have to be rich or live like a king to have an impact on your community and the world around it. The little things that we do every day matter more than most people realize because someone out there is looking for a helping hand just like yours was at one time or another. If you're kind enough to give yours when needed, then others will find their way towards being kind as well. One good deed begets another until the entire world embraces it as one of its own ways of life.

Just remember that change doesn't happen overnight with just one act alone so never stop trying no matter how small or insignificant something may seem. You never know who it might be reaching or how many people may benefit from your actions in the end, no matter how silly they may have seemed at first.

Never underestimate the significance of a kind gesture when it comes to changing someone else's life around for them. It could mean everything when you're willing to set aside your pride and give of yourself without expecting anything in return; no fame, no fortune, not even an acknowledgment that you were there helping someone out in need. Knowing that you made a difference in someone's life will make all the difference for you as well at the end of the day. All it takes is some effort from you.

Right now we are dealing with tense race relations as well as gender identity issues demanding that we recognize a plethora of different personalities or orientations to be fact, not fiction; all while crooked governments around the world sit back and laugh knowing they've helped cause all of this discord while they try to tear us down to our knees from the inside.

You don't have to deal with any of this to be a good

person. You are in control of how people treat you and how they see you. If you help someone without expecting anything in return, that is the definition of love in its purest form. However, no human being can truly love another until they care for themselves first. When we fully understand that the majority of people only act out of self-interest or worse so many times instead; it's important to make sure that your own needs are always met before helping others out.

It takes time and effort to show sympathy for other people who deserve better than what they're getting in life but there is a lack of incentive for those around us at the present moment to do so. When we stop thinking about what other people are doing wrong in their lives and start to focus on all the things they're doing right, that's when real change begins to take place for everyone involved.

It can be so easy to lose track of yourself if you spend too much time obsessing over the crazy shit going on around the world but it doesn't do anyone any good to get caught up with negativity. If there is one thing that today's society has forgotten entirely, it's that charity begins at home before helping others out in any way shape, or form. It's only once you have everything under control within your own mind and surroundings that you'll ever be capable of making a real difference for someone else who might need a helping hand as well.

It's been said over and over again how important self-love is for us to better connect with those around us in all different walks of life. Once you've mastered the art of putting yourself first before anyone else does, then it's time to see what others have done with their lives and give praise where praise is due. If you're willing to look past someone else's flaws or shortcomings then they'll open up towards you showing theirs as well. A little recognition goes a long way when it comes to changing people for the better, but on the flip side, don't let your guard down just because someone can recognize your minor shortcomings. Sometimes that means they know exactly how easy it will be to manipulate you into doing something that may hurt you in the long run.

As an Alpha, it's your job to look past even the most unsavory of people at times and give them grace when they need it most. We can only stare down a horse's ass for so long until we see that we're becoming just as bad as what we're looking at prior to changing our minds about things around us. When someone needs help more than ever, it's time to set aside your own personal interests if only for one minute, and focus on those in genuine need. By doing this, you'll be able to see where your efforts went towards helping another person out that needed assistance the most but was not getting any from anyone else.

When you really stop and think about it, what is money really worth to us outside of our own comfort level? So many times we become too comfortable with having everything handed to us and without the proper work ethic or drive, that's how everyone stays these days. The privilege of living in a first-world country was hard fought for by so many generations before us but now we're almost too soft towards dealing with real pain compared to the hardships our ancestors had to face.

It's very easy to say you've got someone's back when they're winning at life but what happens when they're not? A true Alpha isn't only made during those good times when people try their best or make the right decision; instead, an Alpha shows up and fights even harder for someone who is losing the battle against their own mind and body. You can't look at someone else in a negative way for what they're going through while at the same time give them reasons why you should be helping them with your time, attention, energy, and money.

Once you've successfully helped another person

see their potential once again then it's time to give that level of respect back to other people who need it just as much even if they're not asking for it. This isn't about being condescending towards others because it's obvious there's something wrong (and just how badly) but instead to give back hope toward those who are truly struggling to find the resolve needed to come out on top. If you don't know anything about depression yourself; take some time to learn about it first before you decide to throw out pity towards those whom you think need help the most. Some need it, some just want attention, while others will tell you a story to take advantage of you while your back is turned. Keep your eyes open so you can spot the difference because nothing dims a generous heart more than to have your kindness used against you.

If you want to be successful in life, sometimes you have to realize that some people are going to take advantage of others just because they can. This scenario is not for every person on Earth but there's always a percentage of the population that lives for making other lives as difficult as possible even if they don't have a reason to do so directly. The way an Alpha deals with this is by setting clear boundaries and then sticking to those rules at all times (even when no one else does). By doing this, you'll instantly become a safe haven for any type of person hunted down by their own demons until they come around and finally see things for what they are (before it's too late).

When you find yourself starting to doubt other people's stories about needing your help then that's when it's time to step back and question why you're speaking with those people at all or trying to lend a hand if any part of what they are saying seems off. It might make you feel good knowing that you helped someone but it makes them look bad when they lie just to get something from you like your money or attention. Offer help, not sympathy; try understanding instead of pity, and give advice instead of pointing out the negatives of a situation.

When it comes to giving, don't be nice just so you can get something back but instead do good for others without expecting anything in return. If someone does start expressing gratitude towards you then be humble enough about your actions to know that's all that is needed when there is nothing except pure love behind each gift given.

The world needs good leaders.

The world is in desperate need of good leaders that are not spinning tales and pushing some crooked self-serving agenda put on their desk by special interest groups with very little science and at times none to back up their claims. All of these hinging on a fat payday if they get a fairy tale past the trusting eyes of the voters. Believe nothing you hear and half of what you see is a fine way to apply that brain-crushing treatment to all news that pops up on your computer screen.

Step into the shoes of others before making any rash decisions about life. If someone made an honest mistake then forgive them instead of becoming a person that needs forgiveness in return by their own higher power; you're just as responsible for keeping peace with everyone around you as they are so don't be fooled thinking otherwise. The world needs people who can make themselves humble enough to admit when something has gone wrong (or even right) while at the same time, showing love and respect in equal amounts toward all people no matter how they might look or sound toward them.

A true Alpha will teach and lead by example while not preaching what they are going to do because of their title. A leader doesn't blame others for the bad decisions made or point a finger to distract voters from seeing what is really going on behind the scenes. Being smart enough means keeping your wits around you at all times so you can safely get through life without having everything come crashing down on your head when it's someone else's turn in life to show off how much more power they have than you!

The world needs good leaders. The world is waiting for YOU! OK, so maybe not you, but someone like you. Let's all work together to change the world.

A leader doesn't waste time on trivial things (or thoughts) that are a waste of time in general. The world needs better leaders who can bring people together like you and me, not tear them apart with empty promises or future plans that cannot be accomplished (because the person saying it doesn't even know what they are going to do). When someone is having a hard time getting through life then you should be there for them to help them move up the ladder instead of pushing them down deeper into an endless pit.

The Alpha helps others because, deep down inside, they see themselves in those same shoes as before now standing on top during times when everyone else has given up on their dream. Remember not to believe everything you hear or read. Keep your eyes and ears open for the propaganda that is being shoved down our throats by people who want to be praised like an Alpha, when in reality they are nothing more than a person on autopilot trying to get a pay raise during a time of tough economic times. (Granted it's sometimes hard not to fall into their verbal traps).

The world needs good smart leaders who can think clearly without worrying about how much money they might lose if they turn down a well-planned marketing scheme that won't help people in the long run, just make life difficult. Times are changing and we need change to go with it if we ever want to make this planet better for our children and theirs.

A true Alpha does things from the heart, not the wallet.

A leader doesn't want to be called a leader so

someone can tell them that they are and then when asked about it, start bragging about how much work they did behind the scenes for many years before ever getting elected or appointed into their title. A true leader instead says humbly, "I am only doing what I have been told in my heart is the right thing to do." Because a true Alpha sees others as being more important than themselves or any of their own material things! Just imagine the world that would develop if every person started thinking this way . . . something like an angel on Earth.

The idea is basically "Give first and get second" and make sure you're giving from your heart because it's the right thing to do, not because you want something in return. You can't take it with you when your life ends so why hold onto it for so long if you don't have any plans (or dreams) of using it while you're here?

A true Alpha doesn't care about being rich or popular for status sake alone, as those things don't really matter in the end. Being a charlatan does though once someone drinks their Kool-Aid (or whatever type of sugary political pills they are pushing on you). The world needs people who think independently and aren't influenced by others, but instead able to make their own decisions without having to worry about what everyone else is thinking around them. Why waste your precious time doing things for others when you could be working to pay off your own debt and helping to enrich the lives of those in your own communities? The people in your community don't owe you anything, but their general welfare is still just as much your responsibility as anyone else's. You do not own the Earth nor this country, so please act like it!

An Alpha realizes that life isn't about having all the things or getting everything you can at someone else's expense because they think if they don't then they will never get those same opportunities themselves. The world needs better leaders who lead by example and inspire others to have the confidence in themselves to do more than what has been asked of them because "why not?" A true leader is out there like a beacon with their light shining brightly for everyone else to see, instead of dimmed down low when they think they are out of sight. An Alpha realizes that there is always an opportunity to be a better human being and never gives up on trying to make things work, so if you want to become a leader then start with yourself first!

A gift that is given freely.

A gift that is given freely comes back 10 times in the end; universally speaking of course. People aren't like slot machines; they're not going to shower you in riches for helping them. The universe, however, is like a slot machine in a sense. The more good energy you put in, the more good energy you get back. That's why helping others is the best deal around.

So think of it like this: You give $10 to someone in need, yet you don't ever expect anything back from them because it was your decision to give what you had at that time. If they choose to pay it forward and do something good for someone else then the chain reaction of good energy continues. There is no limit to how much people of this world can be blessed in the end by a simple act of kindness.

An Alpha stops the plight of suffering one person at a time because someone has got to start somewhere! A true leader never thinks it's too trivial if what they are asking you to do is something that affects just two people instead of millions. If each person helps just 2 other people then those 3 will help 6 more and so on until billions are helped and major issues have been solved: world hunger, homelessness...etc. It's called "The Butterfly Effect" and it ties directly into Karma.

An Alpha knows that good things come back to you in the end and it can be in a number of different ways, not just monetary. Sometimes good energy comes back to you in ways that you didn't even know you needed. I can't count the number someone that I didn't even know showed up out of the blue just when I needed help the most. The universe sees you and it likes balance, so a debt never goes unpaid as long as you're open to the method of repayment.

An Alpha is a Leader, Not a Boss

What it really means to be a leader.

A leader is someone that is willing to get their hands dirty right along with the people they lead. They do the things that other people aren't willing to do because they know that if they fail, everyone else around them does as well.

A boss, on the other hand, creates an environment where people feel like they'll be treated better if they just push themselves hard enough. They create an environment where everyone is out for themselves because it's in their best interest to do so. Being a boss makes you a hindrance to your team and will eventually destroy them.

One of the biggest mistakes I've seen leaders make is that they try to keep their distance from the people they want to lead. They create an environment where someone can get promoted into a leadership position without ever having had much experience or earned respect from those that followed them. This does not work out well in the long term and it's something you definitely want to avoid.

An alpha is different, they're someone that has earned the respect of those around them and people look up to them because they are a better version of themselves. They work hard to earn that respect and it shows in everything they do. Not only does everyone love working with an Alpha, but most people love Alpha leaders as well because they don't leave their employees hanging when things go sideways.

An Alpha takes pride in being the hardest worker, they're willing to do whatever it takes and have no problem stepping in wherever needed. They'll put their hands on a shovel along with everyone else when something needs digging and they won't ask anyone else to do the job for them.

An Alpha leads by example. The people that

follow them do so because they want to be better, and the first step is taking a look at what an Alpha does. Watch how they respond in pressure situations. How they handle mistakes and failure. What makes them different from everyone else?

A leader's job is to create an environment where people can improve, not just express fear or doubt in the people they lead. Leadership is about creating an environment where you are willing to learn from someone who knows more than you. It's about letting go and letting those around you become better versions of themselves.

You don't have to be perfect to be a great leader, but being willing to get your hands dirty right along with the people and trust them is a step in the right direction.

Do you really want to succeed?

This is something everyone needs to ask themselves before taking on any new project.

Whether it's financial or personal you need to be willing to put in the long hours to achieve your success and not overlook the important steps because it seems too hard. There's a fine line between pushing yourself to your limits and just repeating the same things over and over because they're easier than being great.

An Alpha never questions whether or not something is worth it, they'd rather die trying than fail before even starting. They know that success can only be achieved if you are willing to work hard and get dirty every step of the way. Why do you think pro football players hit the gym religiously? It's because it's mentally draining to lose. They want to make sure that they come back stronger and better next season, not coming back wondering what they did wrong and why things didn't work out.

The people I respect the most are those who failed but found a way to succeed by learning from mistakes. If you aren't willing to fail then you'll never achieve anything great in life. You have to be able to take risks, chances that might fail before you can find success.

Everyone creates their own failure when they stop trying. It's easy to let your mind convince yourself that something isn't worth your time or just too difficult and it just becomes easier to quit. If you aren't willing to take a chance or get your hands dirty then you'll never be able to succeed in life.

Don't let fear hold you back from becoming the person that you've always wanted to be, but don't fool yourself into thinking it's going to be easy either. Success is challenging and failure is often just around the corner. You're only going to learn how far you can go when you push through the fear to do better than before, so push yourself more, and work harder.

Never stop being someone who is willing to get their hands dirty because those are the people who make things happen in this world. Not everyone will like what they see but it's not their dream, and they need to see you getting after it because if you think it feels bad when they're hating your journey, imagine how amazing it will feel when they get to pout from the sidelines of your success.

Everyone is built differently, but even when we have different bodies and minds, every person can accomplish the same if not better things. What separates them from others is their ability to be open-minded and willing to take a chance on themselves.

If you want something great in life then you're going to have to prove that it's worth the long hours and hard work involved. Those who are willing or put in the effort will arrive at an important milestone faster than people who aren't any different than anyone else except for their willingness to get dirty along with everyone else. The greatest achievement of all is finding someone who has accomplished what you want to do and learning from their mistakes.

The Alpha may not always be the most popular person in the room but they can still be successful even without a following of people around them all the time. In fact, many times those with a large group of followers unknowingly begin to rely on too many people rather than taking charge of their own success plan.

Many people are content to follow others because they feel that someone else has things better figured out than they do so why bother figuring out their own solutions? The truth is there's no right or wrong way to go about it as long as you're willing to put in the work required for your goals.

Just think about what would happen if you were forced to follow someone else plans for a change. How would it feel to be forced into doing what someone else wants rather than taking control over your own life? Change is inevitable for people who are willing to embrace the challenges that come along.

An Alpha doesn't ask permission because they're not afraid of being challenged or upset about how others might feel. They're comfortable in their own skin and able to take charge on their own time without needing approval from anyone else.

If you don't like the way things work then why wouldn't you try creating a new path that leads toward success? You don't have to wait around for other people to create opportunities only available if you follow along behind them, make one of your own instead. It's easier said than done, but so is everything that you want in life.

Don't let anyone threaten your success just because you're taking a different approach than they would have chosen to do. Learn from the best while trying to be better than everyone else even if it means being alone at times. You don't need other people by your side when you've proven yourself to be better than those who have been around for years but are stuck where they are now instead of moving forward on their own progress.

Some people may never be convinced that you are determined to win in life and need to leave old toxic habits behind. You may find that you have to leave some of your old group behind in order for them to realize that they aren't needed anymore because you've grown beyond their skills or outlook about what is possible.

An Alpha doesn't place their success in the hands of others and doesn't wait around for someone to tell them what they can achieve. They know that greatness is often a lonely journey but knowing that they made themselves great is worth the hard work involved all on its own. Getting ahead isn't without obstacles, but with determination, you'll be able to overcome any hurdle in your way.

In life, no one else will do all the work for you and build the path toward real success. Those who are able to make things happen on their own might not be given as much credit by those who have a large entourage but understand that what they've accomplished has taken time, persistence, and hard work.

It doesn't matter how many people are standing at your side when you achieve something great because it was your efforts that made it possible in the first place. The people around you may give compliments about this amazing accomplishment but without your open-mindedness and willingness to break through barriers others wouldn't even know your name at all.

Those who have gone before you may complain that you paved a new road where theirs also used to be, but they should take a moment to think about how far their success was built on someone else's hard work and dedication.

An Alpha realizes the importance of being self-driven even when others might not appreciate it at first. You don't need multiple people putting in their two cents for something to make sense because if you aren't clear on what you want then why not just let others do the thinking for you? They'll be there with an opinion whether you plan out your own future or not so why not work toward something great rather than letting them tell you what is possible?

When nothing is holding success back then you have to learn how to will yourself forward. It won't just fall into your lap without some effort on your part, but those who seek it out are worthy of having their dreams fulfilled in time. If others resent you for taking the lead and building something great then that's not going to stop you from moving forward with confidence about what is possible if you keep pushing ahead each day toward the future that only you can make happen.

A world full of followers isn't going to get anyone anywhere because they're waiting for someone else to do all the work for them while expecting praise when things go well in their lives. An Alpha isn't afraid of doing everything on their own because they know that this is what builds success over time. The people who place blame on others for their unhappiness are just being small-minded and don't have the courage to make real changes in life.

You will be a leader in your own right if you seek out what is possible because there are no limits that can hold you back when you set out to break down barriers that keep others from moving forward. Those who follow may depend on living off of other's accomplishments without really making their own, but an Alpha will look at where things stand today with this new knowledge about how far they can go if they get out of their own way and put their energy into something worthwhile instead of sitting around waiting for things to come easy.

How to be a leader and not just the boss.

    This may sound a bit redundant but it bears repeating because too many businesses fail due to a leader that isn't a leader at all, but just a belligerent boss that barks orders at their subordinates. You'll be a leader when you are ready to take the responsibility for what happens in your own life instead of blaming others or making excuses. A good leader knows how to delegate tasks and pass along responsibilities when needed, but is still able to lead their group just as effectively as before without losing trust because they respect their people by empowering them instead of forcing them into submission through intimidation.

    Real leaders don't need to constantly prove themselves through controlling others. That will only build resentment among those who have been ordered around all day by someone else's every whim whether it's justified or not. If your job involves having people do exactly what you say then maybe management isn't the right career path for you. If you enjoy a challenge and not being stuck in one place then you'll draw people to your side who share the same values as you do, because they will see that working with someone like this is worth their time.

When you have something to prove it can be hard not to take things so seriously sometimes but whatever has happened in the past doesn't determine what will happen in the future. You don't need to live forever with regrets about what has come before just for the sake of justifying current actions against those who might judge them on a superficial level. For every boss that treats their employees poorly, there's going to be some employee that takes this out of context without thinking about how they are contributing toward making life difficult for others through uncooperative actions that they're taking.

When everyone's being an asshole then

nothing gets accomplished and things that started out good eventually fall apart. This is what happens when you leave bad things unsaid between people and let them stew in resentment until it comes out in the form of insults or worse yet some kind of physical confrontation. It may be better to have face-to-face interaction with someone instead of shooting off a message through social media just because you're too scared to call them directly on the phone, but if you do so without getting everything said that needs saying then all this is going to end up doing is making things worse than they needed to be in the first place.

So next time something like this happens make sure that you take responsibility for your own actions and apologize to everyone who has been offended because without them you might not have had the chance to get things moving in the right direction. And if you're not sure how to do this then read up on some self-help books or watch inspirational videos where people can point out ways that they've overcome their obstacles in life to get where they are now. There's no shame in taking an interest in what other people have done, even people you don't know personally, just as long as you don't neglect your responsibilities along with everything else.

What kind of leader would you like to be?

The good news is that anyone can accomplish anything they put their mind to doing if it's something worth getting excited about while at the same time it's incredibly easy to fall into what can only be described as a form of mental laziness. If you didn't work up the courage to ask that special girl out on a date or stopped yourself before making that big career move then chances are your mind has been conditioned in such a way that you're trying to protect yourself from further failure, even though this will likely end up hurting you more than if you had taken those initial chances instead of letting them slip right through your fingers.

But where do you draw the line between being confident and over-confident? It's true that some people who take things too far wind up embarrassing themselves because they've gotten carried away with something they thought would benefit their lives but never turned out quite right. And when you're the life of the party then it's easy to get caught up in all of the hype with friends and forget about who you really are along with what responsibilities need to be handled outside of work or home. The good news is that people can change but the bad news is that you might have to learn some hard lessons before you accomplish this goal.

It's possible to turn lemons into lemonade by simply being willing to try out new things even when they don't wind up turning out exactly as planned at first so long as they still end up being fun at some point down the line. In fact, there are times where someone may take a chance on something and look back later only realizing how much better this made their life in comparison to where they would have been without these types of experiences. And this is easy to take for granted because if you have a family or make it your goal to pay off debt, then the last thing you'll want to do is stop and smell the roses along with everything else that could be going just fine in your life right now.

But if there's one thing every leader needs to remember, more than any other trait out there, it's how important it can be not just to get things done on time but also enjoy what you're doing while at the same time being willing to accept personal responsibility for all of your actions. It's like a job as an employee where someone who has no care about their boss's feelings or just wants to do as little work as possible but gets paid for the same amount as someone who does their best and gets a lot done at the same time. And it can be incredibly easy to fall into this trap because of how tempting it is to not take your boss's words seriously when they tell you that something needs to be handled right away, or in some cases not at all.

But where does passion come from?

I truly enjoy reading personal development books from time to time, especially those that talk about overcoming obstacles that can have a real impact on my life rather than just talking about "fluff" for no reason other than making me feel good about myself. Most of these articles you find online today are just here to make you feel good about yourself because it's hard to find authors who want to get right into the meat and potatoes of what makes people tick.

And if you're someone who often feels discouraged, for whatever reason, then it might be time to forget about what everyone else has told you in the past while at the same time acknowledging that there are plenty of resources out there that can be accessed from home at any given moment but only if you go looking for them. The problem with most self-help books is that they don't provide clear-cut steps on how you can apply everything being said in relation to your own life. But where do you start when even realizing that a problem exists seems like too much work? It's time to stop making excuses for yourself and start seeing the bigger picture, but in a way that doesn't make you feel bad about yourself.

For example, it's easy to blame others who may be responsible for something that went wrong in your life, and there are times where someone might have tried their best but this didn't always end up turning out as planned. If you consider anything outside of your control then this can sometimes be a factor of how much work needs to be done going forward so long as you realize that nothing is set in stone or etched into a rock somewhere. Getting what you want out of life does take some work upfront, especially if this isn't part of everyone's daily routine. But if you don't do the necessary legwork, then all of your efforts are wasted and this can have a real impact on feeling overwhelmed by how much work needs to be done as a result of procrastinating for so long.

    I guess this is my long-winded way of saying, to be a leader and not a boss, you need to care about the people that follow you, not just tell them what to do. You also need to care about yourself and take time to unwind doing the things you enjoy or being around the people you love. An Alpha knows that when you don't take time for self-care and you allow things to build up you will eventually take it out on people that most likely didn't deserve it. Lastly, if you don't feel that you have the skills to accomplish these goals then watch videos, read books, or ask someone that you feel does. A true leader isn't afraid to seek out help or feedback.

Get more done by delegating

It's also important to understand that you don't have to do everything alone. Seek out the people that have the skills to do the tasks you need to get done so you can delegate less important tasks allowing you to focus on pressing issues like investing in the time or skills that can help your project grow or improve the lives of everyone around you.

You already have enough on your plate so start looking to others for help. In most cases, people are willing to help if you only ask them for it. Don't be afraid of rejection and know that even if a person doesn't do what was originally asked of them they might become an invaluable resource in another area of your life or business. You never know until you let things unfold naturally.

There is no "one-size-fits-all" approach to leading; you can't just use the same methods that worked for someone else and expect them to work with your team. Each team brings its own set of problems to solve but they also have a unique way of doing things. So stop trying to be like everyone else and start creating your own unique style or method depending on what works best for you and those that follow you in life.

I'm sure this isn't new information, but it's also important to keep in mind that people are stubborn! Once they've been told how something should be done by someone they respect, then it's hard for them to come up with outside-the-box ideas on how to do something differently. So just because someone said or did something one way, doesn't mean that this is how it should always be done. You need to experiment and understand if the status quo is truly better than what you have in mind before trying to implement your own ideas into practice. In other words, don't fix what isn't broken unless you know for sure you can improve upon it.

How to lead your team without

micromanaging

Be available for your team whenever they need you but don't be constantly looking over their shoulder. Trust them to get the job that you need them to do done, but don't expect them to always do it exactly the way you showed them how. I take pride in seeing each team I lead expand on the lessons I have taught them, especially when I see them improve upon my methods because it teaches me valuable lessons I may not have learned otherwise. Just because you're the leader doesn't mean you know everything.

One thing I have learned is it's just as important to know when not to step in and offer help as it is knowing when to jump in the fire. If someone on your team has a problem that they can't solve on their own without some guidance or if you feel like they need more feedback then that's one thing. But no one likes to be micromanaged so don't try managing tasks people are already good at or enjoy doing themselves. People thrive when they're given freedom that motivates them. You will only succeed by giving them opportunities for growth!

Treating your team with respect isn't a sign of weakness; it shows them you care about their opinions even if they aren't capable of doing what you have asked of them. People want to feel important and that they can trust someone with their thoughts, so don't shut them down when they offer a suggestion on how to improve your team or business.

Most people I see within an organization want to be more than just worker bees. If you give them the chance then most will rise up and become leaders themselves in the future; maybe not now but eventually as long as you care about their development instead of managing tasks for them! Don't take away opportunities from your team because it's good for you when someone else is doing something and allowing you to focus on the growth of a project, not just the day-to-day tasks. Eventually, this type of mentality will only hurt everyone involved! Step back and let someone else take the reins when you can.

Why leaders are so important

Most people need leaders in their lives, whether that be role models they can look up to or innovators they can follow toward success. A good leader is someone who can be both a friend and take charge when they need to. It's important for leaders to show teamwork, loyalty, and honesty in all that they do.

You don't have to know everything or even lead everyone on your team to achieve success. But you should always strive to make the people around you better than they were before you helped them out with some advice or guidance. Leaders set the example for how others should act within an organization; they are problem solvers and have the ability to get others excited about new opportunities while opening doors of possibilities.

A true leader isn't one that will just tell others what needs doing but also help those around him/her out as much as possible by taking initiative when needed. Leadership isn't given, it's earned by those who want to be a part of something bigger than themselves. It's important to work hard and show others that you're willing to do anything for them as long as they have your back just the same!

Every leader should have an open-door policy but still leave time for themselves and their families; there is no one size fits all when it comes to leading someone. Everyone has a different way of life with varying personalities so finding what works best for each individual will help you along the way!

I cannot stress enough how important it is for leaders to understand the needs of others. I have seen leaders make great strides in helping those around them with different issues but then struggle once their responsibilities were not met, even if that was out of their control. Leaders need to learn how to adapt and be flexible when situations arise out of their hands.

Being a leader should never be viewed as a responsibility you dread; instead, take each day as a new lesson on how to better yourself while caring about everyone else at the same time! You may not always agree with what people do or say but remember that they are just following your example as someone they look up to or respect because you lead by example!

If you want to reach your goal and build a legacy then you have to learn how to lead others toward that same goal. Let your team see how hard you work and what sacrifices you are willing to make on their behalf, never forget that they will be doing the same for you, so always take care of them just as much as yourself!

So ask yourself these questions; do I deserve my title? Do I have confidence in myself? Am I someone who can change their bad habits or someone who only wants others to change instead of me first? If not then maybe you aren't cut out for leadership but instead are meant to be a follower.

If you want others to respect you and follow your example then you have to first prove that it's worth their time, effort, and energy for them to do so! Use your past experiences in life as guidance toward leading those around you; take each day as a new opportunity on how to help yourself while helping everyone else at the same time. Don't forget why you wanted to become a leader in the first place, only then will people begin looking up to what you represent! If I had one thing I could tell all leaders no matter what position they hold within an organization it would be: Your legacy is built every day by the actions that you make or don't make. Be known for something great!

Everyone enjoys being led when they know they are becoming a part of something greater than themselves. So think about what you need to do to build your legacy, not only within your job or organization but also in life! Once you start helping others and changing some of the bad habits that hold you down then maybe you'll find yourself on a leadership track that will land you somewhere big. Just remember — never give up because "you can" change all those bad habits into good ones one step at a time and become the leader that inspires others to change their own.

How to be a leader in your life

Be a leader by stepping up and doing the things that other people aren't willing to do. There are too many people that make up endless excuses as to why they can't get ahead, or get the job done, or save the relationship, or countless other "I can't" statements. I have to fight the urge on a daily basis to turn my nose up at these people because the negativity is almost an unpalatable stench at times. Don't be like those people; stand up and push through because there is no excuse for failure when you didn't really try to begin with.

Just because a lot of your friends and family may not agree with what you want to accomplish doesn't mean that it's not possible, or can't be done! If you want something bad enough then nothing will stop you from eventually getting there. Just remember — stand up for what is important to you and stay true to yourself so others will respect the path that you have chosen in life.

If you want to stand out from the rest of your peers then maybe you need to seek out a new challenge that will help you build up your confidence along with some great experience. You never know what is waiting for you at the next corner so why not turn the page and get started on the adventure of a lifetime? Do something different, step outside of your comfort zone and see what happens!

Do you know how important it is to embrace each day as a new opportunity? Maybe just maybe, if given the chance, you can turn an obstacle into an opportunity instead of letting it hold you down. You have two choices: whine about why something isn't working or go out and fix it instead. How many times do we hear people say things like "oh I tried that before" — when in reality they never really even gave their best effort! So start today by fixing some problems that are holding you down because there is no time like the present to turn your life upside down and inside out for the betterment of everyone around you!

Don't let anyone tell you what you can or cannot do with your life because at the end of the day it's all up to you. The sooner you accept that responsibility then the sooner you'll see what a person can truly accomplish when they put their mind to it! Be an inspiration to others by showing them that anything is possible through hard work, dedication, and passion for life.

No matter how old we get there will always be

something new and exciting waiting for us out there in the world of tomorrow so why not start today by finding those things? Do something different than what everyone else is doing — go hang gliding, or sky diving, or whitewater rafting, etc. Life gets boring if you don't have enough new experiences each year so make sure you are living an adventure and taking advantage of this great opportunity that we all have called "life".

An Alpha Is A Warrior And Will Not Run

The only way to get through your day is to be a warrior

There is more than one way to be a warrior and it's not all battle cries, the clashing of blades, or gory combat; but if I'm being honest, wouldn't that make people rethink a lot of the ways they treat others. What I'm speaking of though is determination. The willingness to see things through to the end, whether it is finding a positive resolution to a problem or just getting the job done even when no one is helping you out. It's the willingness to put yourself out there, expose yourself, take a chance on failure all while still knowing that you are capable of succeeding.

You must understand though that being a warrior means more than just being brave and strong. It also means that you will stand up for what's right and rage against what's wrong. You will not be pushed around either by other people or your own insecurities – you are strong enough to face anything that may come your way. You value yourself and you won't let anyone tear you down for being who you are. You stand up for those who can't do it themselves but recognize the power that they have within them to make positive changes.

In order to be a warrior, you must rid yourself of the idea that giving up is okay. It's not and it never will be, so stop making excuses for why you can't do something or face your fears. Stop saying that you aren't ready or equipped to deal with life's challenges because if there wasn't a doubt in your mind, you wouldn't be facing it in the first place. If you are truly willing to face that challenge then do it now without hesitating or giving yourself more time to plan out what to say or do. Just go for it!

The only way to survive life is by not wasting time with excuses and just getting on with the task at hand. Being a warrior means believing in yourself even when others don't. You are going to make the right decision, face your fears and fight for what's right. It doesn't matter who is on your side or where they stand because if you truly believe in something then it will happen! Stop procrastinating about getting things done or making the right decisions. Start making positive changes in your life because you are going to be the one left standing due to your belief in yourself.

A warrior knows that it is okay to feel fear and doubt but doesn't let it consume or destroy them. They choose to face their fears, tackle them head-on and prove that they are capable of doing what is necessary even when things go wrong or get out of control. A warrior goes all in and never turns back because they know that there is no point in regretting a decision once it has been made, just don't dwell on things for too long and learn from your mistakes – use them as motivation for doing something different next time around. You cannot change the past but you can be sure that you can change the future. Don't be afraid to trust your instincts and go with it even if others don't agree. You have made your decision because that's what a warrior does; they make decisions and stand by them.

Sure, you may get some flack for being tough-minded but it is better than being easily swayed and making poor choices in haste or anger without giving things much thought. Recognize who you are dealing with though and how they react when faced with confrontation or obstacles. There are people out there who will try everything in their power to break you down so they can finish things off themselves and get ahead before you – so never let them see you sweat! Be strong-minded as well as physically strong so that no one can take advantage of you.

Traits of a warrior include courage, bravery,

self-motivation, the ability to focus, and determination that drive them to make things happen on their own terms. A warrior has no room for excuses because those who make halfway decisions are never really committed to anything.

A warrior doesn't run away from challenges or think about how they can avoid doing something uncomfortable – if it needs to be done then do it! They don't look at things as impossible, they simply go in head first, tackle whatever is put in front of them, and prove that nothing is impossible unless you let it stop you from moving forward. If you always run from your problems and responsibilities instead of dealing with them then what do you expect? That's not being a warrior; that's being a coward and Alphas are not cowards.

How to deal with stress

A warrior does not run but a warrior can feel stress, and the truth is that you need to deal with that stress before your fight or flight response becomes too much to handle. You need to engage in the activities that bring you peace and happiness so you can be at your best when situations arise that need your full attention and unwavering strength. Take time out to relax, meditate, go for a walk in nature or spend time with family and friends. Those who are truly brave know that it's okay to care about others and have fun doing it. They also know that there is no point in living your life in regret by dwelling on things you cannot change – if something needs doing then just do it!

It is important to remember that you never know how strong you are until being strong is the only choice you have left. You must pick yourself up when times get rough but don't drag yourself down by letting your past control every moment of your existence; live as though each day were your last so that you can make the most out of each one because we never really know what is around the corner.

A warrior knows how to face their fears and even if they are standing alone they do not back down from a challenge because they know that there is something waiting on the edge of uncertainty for them. They don't always get it right but those who learn from their experiences will eventually figure out what works best for them so give it your best shot! In the end, you only have yourself to rely on – no one else is going to take care of you because you must learn early on how to be strong in order to survive.

Nothing is impossible unless we make excuses for why we cannot do things when faced with challenges or responsibilities. If everything seems hopeless then try harder! A warrior learns from other's mistakes as well as from their own – they are not the type to ignore what has happened in the past because it will only happen again if you let it. This is why you must find time to destress so you can see things clearly and learn how not to make the same mistakes in the future. You cannot change your mistakes unless you have learned from them and that is how to become a warrior who makes less of them.

A battle can be won or lost before even being fought, which means that you need to know yourself as well as those around you so there will be no surprises when things come up. A warrior takes the time to learn more about themselves and others while keeping an open mind so they will always stay strong mentally as well as physically. A warrior doesn't run away from their problems and responsibilities but instead tackles them head-on – if something needs to be done then do it!

How to be more confident in yourself

Confidence is built over time through trial, error, and success. Don't expect to get it right the first time every time but be sure you learn what went wrong so you can get it right the next time. The more you work at a task the better you will become and in turn, your confidence will follow. Likewise, don't turn away from something just because you've never done it. How else are you going to learn unless you face it like a warrior and push through?

Anyone can learn to be confident and anything is possible if you open your mind. There are no limits to how strong, happy, or successful you can become as long as you keep working towards it. Be open to different points of view when faced with something new so that you can see things in a whole new light – this will help clear the path ahead for achieving whatever goal you may have put out there for yourself.

A warrior doesn't let their fears control them, they don't dwell on their past mistakes because they already know what not to do next time around, but they also make room for fun and relaxation too so that every day doesn't feel like a battle. Yes, stress is inevitable but managing how we respond to it makes all the difference and less stress leads to more confidence.

A warrior doesn't need to run from things that come up in their life because they handle it without panicking – this is how to be a confident person who gets the job done.

If you want something then go after it! A warrior knows what they want and will do whatever it takes to get there. They don't sit around making excuses but instead take action so that they can reach any goal no matter how big or small. Once a challenge is ahead of them, a warrior faces all that comes at them head-on until they achieve what they went after. Each obstacle along the way will build your strength and confidence which means you are more likely to face something else with confidence than fear. If you see an opportunity then grab hold of it, but don't run away from challenges either.

A warrior is as strong mentally as they are

physically and knowledge is power. There will be information that you have to learn in order to pass a class or get the job done because it gives you knowledge that can help when faced with an obstacle. A book is like a sword – you need to learn how best to wield one so you may take advantage of any opportunities presented before your eyes. If there's something new then read up on it beforehand so that you can make the most of your time with whatever it may be and use what little time you have wisely. Knowledge is the ultimate power that builds confidence because when you know something for certain then there is no reason to raise a question as to whether or not you can handle it.

How to get a raise without any prior experience

The best foolproof way to get a raise without having any prior experience in your chosen field is trial by fire, meaning prove yourself by getting things done efficiently while exceeding expectations. No one can question your value when you display how valuable you are. What are you going to do in order to prove your worth? Are you willing to jump headfirst into the fire?

Practice makes perfect. – Not much else needs to be said about this. Do something repeatedly until it becomes natural; it's called a habit for a reason and good ones lead to good results. Doing things that have already been proven effective will help build your confidence because now you know it works, but always try to do things better than the last time around just like an exercise.

Doing anything well takes practice and the more you work at something, the better you'll get at it. There are no exceptions to this rule, so if there is something that you want to learn then dedicate time to learning how to do it until you've mastered your craft. The only way to gain confidence in something is through experience which can be gained by practicing time after time – eventually, these actions become natural.

The truth is you should never expect a raise without any experience. That's called having a sense of entitlement and an Alpha as well as a warrior knows that you never get something for nothing. You should get fair compensation for the work you put in but you can't expect to show up and get paid the same as the person that's been there for 10 years putting in their time to perfect their craft. If you want to get paid the same as the guy at the top then learn to perform your job like the guy at the top...or better if you can.

How to handle a difficult confrontation/conversation.

Always try to find a peaceful resolution if at all possible. Nothing is worth the consequences that come with making rash decisions because someone got under your skin and caused you to act irresponsibly. Talk it out, find a mediator, walk away until cooler heads can prevail, but whatever you do, don't let it escalate to violence, and just to clear up any possible questions; removing yourself calmly from a volatile situation is not running away, it's strategic. In a fight you always have the option of making a strategic retreat; it's easier and less damaging to regroup at a later time rather than to rush headfirst into the unknown without planning. Often times talking to someone later after things have calmed down is more productive than getting wrapped up in the heat of the moment. That's what emotions are for, they're reminders that we need to take breaks from these discussions when our blood starts boiling because it prevents us from knowing how best to handle things. We can use reason as an influence instead of pure emotion which can often lead people astray.

    Don't be afraid to walk away from any confrontation where both parties involved have already said their piece, and don't allow yourself or others around you to get to a point where violence is the only option. If you feel as though someone has wronged you then take time to think over what just happened so that you don't repeat the same mistakes in the future.

It's not running away when it's a strategic retreat because situations can change at any given time and knowing when to walk away makes more sense than getting caught up in the moment, especially because there are no prizes for showing how tough or angry you are. Use your head!

When something goes wrong, look into who is responsible and hold them accountable. Don't act arrogant and immediately say "It wasn't me." Show your accountability by taking responsibility for any actions that may have been your fault; this proves that you're trustworthy while also preventing others from capitalizing on any dishonesty. An Alpha always will take responsibility for their actions as well as the consequences of those actions, even if it is a grudging apology. Move on from that situation and don't dwell on the past because nothing good can come from reliving negative situations; instead, you should use any lessons learned to move forward with your life.

Make sure that you're personally satisfied with your performance before moving on to something new. While you can't control other people's emotions or reactions, you can control whether or not the outcome was successful in other people's eyes; so make sure that what you do makes an impact. Don't waste time and energy only to see things undone by others around you who also want to make their mark in the world and have no problem pointing out your mistakes to get ahead.

Always be truthful and give respect where it's due. An Alpha doesn't have to put people in their place but they know how to do so whenever the situation calls for it. However, an Alpha will never disrespect someone who doesn't deserve such treatment regardless of how much you may dislike them. Never stoop down to a level that you're not comfortable with; only use strength if it is your right or if no one else will stand up for what's right.

Whatever your reasons might be, never run away from a confrontation in which you are involved as an active participant. It's okay to walk away from something that may cause conflict because there are always other opportunities out there; however, don't leave behind bad blood and don't let a chance at something better slip away. Hold your head up high and face whatever may come with the confidence that you have made the right choices along the way; this keeps you on track as an Alpha while also preventing anyone else from using what was said against you.

Stop running away from the life you deserve.

One of the greatest things that pains me

when I talk to people is their stories of all the missed opportunities. "If I had only done this", or "If I had only said that." It makes me wonder why so many people coast through life never taking the time to go after the things that they are passionate about and bring them joy.

An Alpha has a fire inside them. They want to accomplish things that they know will bring happiness and joy into their lives. Running away from something, instead of going after it brings about feelings that are hard to get over. The guilt of the "what-ifs" can make people miserable when they could be living fulfilling lives full of new experiences.

It's not as difficult as some might think to find fulfillment in life if you just look for it. Once an Alpha finds out what makes them happy, then it becomes easier to make decisions that lead them down the path to their ultimate goals and desires; but first, they have to take a step back from all of the distractions in their lives which only serve to allow others time to point out their weaknesses.

An Alpha is a warrior and will not run from challenges whether they are physical or daily responsibilities. They take the time to know what it takes to be successful at all that they try to accomplish, then learn as much as possible about how to approach their goals in the most efficient manner. This allows them to put forth more effort and energy into whatever they want because the right mindset has been gained so that success isn't an issue but just another step along the way toward perfection.

A lot of people look at life through rose-colored glasses. They believe that everything works out for those who work hard enough and always land on their feet no matter what happens; but this isn't true at all, especially for Alphas. They learn how to be successful at their endeavors by not taking no for an answer and doing whatever it takes to succeed. Your family, friends, and co-workers may try to tell you that you couldn't make this happen or accomplish that task; but if something is truly meant for you then nothing will stop you from getting there.

Never let anyone use excuses in attempts to bring you down or get in your way of achieving your goals. Those who continue on the path of success with strong determination find any obstacles as mere bumps along the way that could have been anticipated and prepared for ahead of time. Those who decide to give up because life dealt them a bad hand are never known as Alphas because they allow even the smallest problems to become bigger than they have to be.

An Alpha doesn't waste time trying to prove to anyone else that they can accomplish great things. They're not worried about what others might think, nor do they care if someone tries to tell them they are doing the wrong thing by following their dreams. Without making decisions based on what others want or expect, you will find yourself enjoying a much happier life than you ever could when caving in and giving up on your goals.

The Alpha never runs from a challenge because they know that every obstacle and problem is just another opportunity for them to learn how to overcome new obstacles. The emotions of guilt, fear, or doubt should not be allowed to overwhelm the person who is confident in their abilities; because knowing that you are one step closer to your success when overcoming an issue, then allows you to move on and tackle the next goal without hesitation.

Whenever someone encounters something new about themselves, don't allow them to run away from everything else around them. It takes guts and courage for someone to deal with what's going on inside of them, but this inward journey must continue if they want to become successful at anything I talk about in this book. Whether you're trying to lose weight or get in shape, dealing with an addiction, or overcoming a break-up; if you allow yourself to look at the situation through your own eyes instead of those of others then everything will make more sense.

The only reason why someone would want to run away from their problems is that they're too afraid to find solutions to them. An Alpha knows that there's never anytime for excuses and that it's up to them alone as to whether they succeed or fail. They refuse to spend too much time thinking about what someone else might think about certain things going on in their lives, nor do they care if family and friends are criticizing their choices.

An Alpha doesn't run from challenges. They fight their way toward them, accept whatever comes their way, and then tackle those things in the most efficient manner. They realize they can overcome any obstacle that someone tries to place in front of them because nothing is too difficult or life-threatening when you truly believe in yourself.

Stop running away from the life you deserve and go after it. Get pumped! Get angry if you have to, but don't make any more excuses and go become the best version of yourself that you can be!

An Alpha Can't Submit

This chapter is more about the psychology behind being an Alpha. The framework that makes up who we are spiritually, mentally, and emotionally. Physical stature aside, what makes a true Alpha is the willingness to do what others won't and the sheer iron will that makes you seemingly unbreakable under pressure. A true Alpha not only won't submit; they can't submit.

Why an Alpha can't submit

Being an Alpha is more of a spiritual calling than a choice. It is something that has been there since the day you were born and though it may have only shown up in small ways for most of your life, there will come a time when you won't be able to deny what you are... or you'll just grow comfortable being looked at as an asshole. Nothing could be further from the truth for those of us that walk the path in the right way but we have no qualms with the title if it gets the job done.

Interestingly enough, the Alpha mentality tends to be something that is recognized at an early age. Hell, you may have even been called a 'leader' or a 'natural born leader' when you were still in diapers. You know your stuff and though there are plenty of people who try to tell you differently, you've always known better - about everything from how best to pour the most perfect sandcastle on the beach (mound it up just right) to how important it is to get your opinion out before anyone else can present one that makes no sense but still somehow leads the masses down the completely wrong path. Although you probably didn't learn the actual importance of speaking up until after childhood.

When we're talking about Alphas, submission isn't really on the table as anything other than a temporary learning experience; a way of feeling the sense of submission long enough to hit that natural gag reflex letting you know you absolutely detest the idea. This is part of the reason that Alphas can't submit. Submission is something that comes from a place inside an Alpha that doesn't exist. They simply don't have the fight or flight response that causes others to cower in fear. An Alphas fight or flight response is to primarily fight all threats unless we are moving off to a strategic position to gain better ground to fight all threats. An Alpha knows that everything has a weakness which means that if it's a threat it can be beaten or overcome if it's just a challenge.

An Alpha can do just about anything else on earth but submitting is not on the list of things that they can comfortably do. It's on par with 'growing another head' or 'shooting lasers from their nipples'. It's just not going to happen and it's not even something you can expect them to try if they've already told you that they are an Alpha. Although the lasers from the nipples thing would be pretty cool if they could.

An Alpha knows what they want out of life, how to get there, and exactly who they need at their side but unfortunately for them (as far as relationships are concerned) they need something that's even harder to find. The world of social media and mainstream media has taught people that everyone can be a leader and we are all equals. On the cosmic/spiritual level, this is true in many ways, but the even more truthful representation of people as a whole is that most will eventually crumble under pressure and have no business leading the way because they will end up taking the rest down with them. Most people by nature are followers whether they want to admit it or not and they have a horrible tendency of following morons because someone on the internet or the news told them it was the best choice.

I understand this is a very cynical and most times unpopular view of the world as a whole but all one has to do in most cases is just watch people for a while; the truth will jump out and bite you on the nose. It is a very unfortunate aspect of the human condition that we have to endure. Some people will never change no matter how many times they hit the brick wall in life, and ignorance is the shield of an arrogantly weak person. If they always refuse to listen to the facts that they never knew in the first place then they can stand on their soapbox and scream about how right they are in the faces of those that disagree with their insanity.

This more than ever is why an Alpha can't submit. We refuse to be led blindly down a dark path that we didn't research first, at least enough that we kind of have an idea of where it's going. If you always believe the first thing that's put in front of you because you don't want to offend the crowd of morons screaming at you to give in then you only have yourself to blame when it all falls apart and you didn't have a lifeline to pull yourself out. We are the ones that see the cliff and turn the other way while the rest of the lemmings leap to their doom. Better yet, if we're lucky and did enough research, we'll be sitting high up on a branch with a box of popcorn, safely watching the carnage while we plan our next move.

The meaning of submission

To some submission can feel like it has negative connotations. While it is something that an Alpha cannot do, for the most part, it doesn't have to be negative. Everything when looked at from the right perspective can be positive. When you look at submission as just giving in and being broken then you are living it in a negative. To me, true submission simply means submitting to your place in life. We need good leaders in this world, but we also need good followers.

This doesn't mean those that follow blindly, although in some cases you may have no other choice; but we need those that work toward the common good because they know that if we all work together, then we all benefit. When everyone is vying for the top position and no one is listening to the person that's already there, then nothing gets done and it all falls apart. Some people, quite frankly just need to learn when to shut up and get back to work. Just because, in your opinion, you can do it better, doesn't mean that you can, and sometimes you're just the asshole standing in the way of everyone else having a good day.

Not everyone can lead the pack, but everyone plays their part. Supporting roles are sometimes the best roles too because an Alpha needs those that follow them to advise them of the things they don't see. Being an Alpha doesn't mean knowing everything, we have people for that, but it means being able to do what others can't with the information provided and being willing to make the hard choices others won't or have the will to stay the course when others would turn away. We need to have an Alpha at some point in our lives, or else we all get lost.

No matter how much you may hate it, being an Alpha is a completely different level of a person that is willing to put aside ego, fear, and sometimes their own personal happiness (albeit momentarily) for the good of the whole. It's what makes us strong as a community and allows people to live their life without worrying about someone stepping on their toes. When everyone knows where they stand with one another then everything is smooth sailing. Without an Alpha though, there's no clear line of command and every decision that needs to be made gets passed down from each level leaving the chain very disjointed. If there were no Alpha, then who would be in charge?

There has to be someone at the helm making those hard decisions that others don't and no amount of utopian garbage about the collective consciousness or everyone's opinions mattering is going to change that. Some people have shitty ideas and while their contribution is still important in life, their ideas, not so much. When you live in a community, the Alpha is there. It doesn't matter if they are the head of a charitable organization, a benevolent dictator, or whatever else people like to label them as; they are still there and everyone knows it. That's why they call it the top because someone has to be calling the shots otherwise things fall apart.

This doesn't mean that a submissive person can't call the shots and go on to be very successful, but a submissive person needs someone to turn to at some point in their daily life for guidance or support. That person is usually an Alpha of some sort. Whether it's a parent, a relative, a friend, a partner, or an investor/consultant that has helped get you to where you are and advises you how to stay there; some people need that person that keeps them steady and sees them through the rough patches.

So, what does that all mean then? Does it mean that if you are a true Alpha, you can't be docile around the right people? Well, no not at all, but that's usually why you need the right partner be it romantic or a mutually beneficial business relationship. Being an Alpha means being able to lead almost by default but sometimes the best follower is the one that has previously led. It doesn't matter whether they call themselves a Beta or an Omega (although I do prefer those terms in some respects, wink, wink) there are times when everyone needs someone to listen to their problems or take them out for coffee and give them advice on how to handle a situation they never thought about before. While we need Alphas for very important reasons, and sometimes only another Alpha can advise an Alpha, we desperately need the supporting roles for comfort, friendship, and a gentler form of guidance; not just those that carry out orders and keep the machine running smoothly.

All I'm saying here is don't discount the role that everyone plays in our day and age. Just because you're an Alpha doesn't mean you can't find a well-suited Beta or Omega that gives you comfort when you need it or provides the guidance to get you back on track. Sometimes, being an Alpha means knowing when to follow someone else for a short period of time so you can learn the lessons they have to teach. Everyone plays role in life, but an Alpha's role is a heavy one and they need the support of those around them. Don't ever look down on those that can't do the things you do because there will come a time when you need them to lift the two things that you might never be able to lift on your own; your heart and your soul.

How I discovered my true Alpha nature

Mine has always been an interesting path and one that separates me from those around me, as does the path of most true Alphas. We are unique as is everybody but an Alphas strength surpasses the rest.

I always fear telling this story because I get the funny looks that tell you everyone thinks you're nuts unless I'm talking to a group of mediums or native Americans who understand the path I'm on.

When I was three is when I had my first encounter with the spirit realm or another dimension, I'm not sure where these beings were from. I woke up in the middle of the night and my bed was surrounded by the spirits of wolves that walked on two legs. Males, females of all ages filled my room. I was terrified at first until I realized they didn't mean me any harm. It felt like they were welcoming me to this world/plane of existence and after this ceremony of sorts was over they slowly filed out and back into the ether. All except one that stayed a moment longer. A female pup that was possibly my soulmate yet to be born at the time giving me one last look and a see you soon feeling.

That's just speculation of course. This is something that has stuck with me throughout my entire life though.

The wolves began guiding me through my dreams and even popped up at key points on the earthly plane as warnings of danger. One such time was when I was driving back from southern Oregon over Mt Hood in the middle of the night. It was foggy and I couldn't see anything while I was coming through the pass. Suddenly there was a break in the fog, and in the sky was a cloud formation shaped like a howling wolf. It caught my eyes and made me hyper-aware just in time to round the corner and see an avalanche that had come out over the road. I was able to react with enough time to correct my steering as the truck skidded toward the embankment, heading for the cliff as I skirted around the rocks and back onto the highway heading toward home.

Circumstances like these have littered my life

and made me understand beyond a shadow of a doubt that there is greatness in store. How much, I'm not sure, but great nonetheless and soon to be discovered. It has led me to understand that nothing should ever be taken for granted and all things in life are sacred with lessons to teach if you are open to learning. They have taught me to never back down from the situations or the people that cause you adversity because there are always brighter days right on the other side of all the nonsense.

Life is not always going to be easy but if it were you probably wouldn't learn much from it. We are given choices and if you make the wrong one, the choice will come back around but the next time will hurt more each time you screw it up; an Alpha grows each time.

I have been beaten, stabbed, shot at, hit by cars, cheated on by almost everyone I opened my heart to, taken for granted, and used more times than I can count, but none of it has stopped me, broken me, or made me quit. I have watched friends descend into alcohol addiction, drug addiction, and seen too many take the final fall into darkness with suicide. It has left me screaming to the sky at times, "Why me? What makes me different?" and there is only one answer, besides the cosmic destiny yet to be told. That answer is, I am an Alpha and I do not break!

An Alpha Embraces Their Own Humanity

An Alpha may be different from those around them and better at things that others are not but it does not make them above humanity. It means they play an important role in leading, guiding, protecting, and standing up for humanity when others turn away. It also means understanding that they are human and need a support structure just as much as they are needed for support. It would do many people well, Alpha or not, to remember this. We all need each other and no one is less valuable than the next.

The importance of understanding your own humanity and why you need to embrace it.

You need to understand your own humanity because there are too many people in this world that walk around like they can do no wrong and like they're going to live forever, neither of which is true.

It's also true to state that most people who walk through life acting like they don't need anyone are actually the ones that need people the most at times. It's the ones that try to be independent and strong when they really aren't who are the most likely to crumble in a crisis. It's why it would do us all some good to remember the importance of being human with each other, especially in a world where we're surrounded by things designed to make us forget about our own humanity.

There are so many reasons that you should embrace your own humanity; one of which is that it will help draw others out of the darkness. When people look at someone who is vulnerable or shows humanity they're more likely to open up about their own insecurities than fear any repercussions for doing so. It's easier to have empathy when you're feeling similar emotions because it reminds us we aren't above anyone else, not even those who seem superior. It's also why a true leader can show their own human side without fear of reprisal or loss of respect.

A good Alpha understands personal responsibility and isn't afraid to take it on when the time comes. They are well-grounded in their own humanity and they aren't afraid to admit that they have needs like anyone else. This type of person is grounded enough to realize if someone needs help or has a problem then it's up to them and others who want progress within a group to step up and do something about it. A mature Alpha knows that there aren't any problems in life that can't be solved with cooperation, compassion, and commitment from all parties involved; even those they see as enemies.

The most important thing to remember when trying to be more human in a world that's forgotten what it means is that you have to feel it first. It's why many people have this idea that an Alpha is so different from others because they're cold and heartless, neither of which is true. They simply understand that there are lines between right and wrong and don't allow feelings to cloud their judgment. It doesn't mean an Alpha doesn't feel anything but if they do then they learn how to not let those emotions affect them too much or take over completely like anger or revenge. If emotion is allowed to rule them as though they were just another animal fighting for dominance in the animal kingdom then what's the difference between a human Alpha and an angry dog?

It takes practice but everyone can do it, even those who feel like they were put on this earth to rule; anyone can change. It just means learning how to not let your emotions control you and as long as you're willing to try there is immense joy in embracing that which makes us human. It also gives you a lot of opportunities to make friends and leave people better off than when you found them.

Many Alphas forget their own humanity by focusing too much time on physical perfection or some material thing that doesn't make them different from anyone else at all. Many take pride in their physical prowess and combat ability to the point where they start to think their human frailties have no bearing in their lives. The truth is that even Alphas need things like food, water, and comfort but instead of turning to others for help they go out and hunt for it on their own.

An Alpha should be strong enough to know their weaknesses and if you find yourself needing help it's a sign that your human side has caught up with you which doesn't make you any less of an Alpha; it actually means the opposite. It means that you're willing to admit when there are things outside of your control affecting your life because it shows maturity as well as understanding how important humanity really is.

It's why many people who call themselves Alphas are so petty and think they're above the rules that apply to everyone else like not killing others just because you want to. It's why there is this stigma about their kind being cold-hearted and uncaring or out for violence instead of love, loyalty, friendship, honor, respect; all of which are human emotions that would make them less than an animal if they couldn't feel it. It's also why many of these people aren't Alphas at all, just a scared and diminished fraction of what an Alpha really is.

What you need to know about mental health and the Alpha community

Don't listen to society when they say that the Alpha doesn't exist because to do so is to deny who you are. They want you to submit to their toxic and misguided views because opposition to their weak viewpoints makes the world wake up to how foolish some people are. When you submit to weak people it causes anxiety, depression, fits of inner turmoil or rage from the beast inside screaming to be let out and it does a disservice to those around you who so desperately need a sound mind to shed some light on all that is wrong in today's society.

It's toxic to try to shed who you are because you want to try to fit in with people that could never live life on your level, and why would you want to. They fear what they don't understand, and they hate that which they can never attain. Not because they don't have all of the same opportunities at their disposal but because when they see adversity they crumble while playing the victim. When an Alpha meets adversity they bare their teeth and say "Bring it on!"

Don't give in to the fear of being hated by those who can only hate you from a distance while praising someone else for all that you have accomplished. These people are not your friends, they never will be and anyone telling you otherwise is trying to tear down your success or make themselves feel better for being a follower instead of a leader.

Grandmothers and Mothers used to tell their

children to "Be like Mike," but what does that really mean. Who's Mike? Michael Jordan was an Alpha who had the courage to try new things even though it meant making mistakes along the way; he had such determination because when he fell he stood right back up with no hesitation at all. If we take this lesson away from him then it's saying that if we take a fall we should get right back up and keep going.

 Nowadays it's not socially acceptable to tell your children to strive for more or work hard for the things you want in life because making and learning from your mistakes is no longer something to aspire to because it could hurt your feelings. God forbid they fall and get a boo-boo or find out that participation trophies don't exist in the real world. People seem to forget that most of those great athletes or business executives were once just kids who grew up in neighborhoods full of crime only for them to rise above and become better than everyone else. You can't do that if you're afraid to make mistakes or if you're told all your life that you don't have to give it your all because there will always be someone there to flip the bill for your life. An Alpha knows that embracing your mistakes or your weaknesses is part of your humanity along with finding the strength within to get back up to fight through and move forward.

Is there a role for compassion in leadership?

Why do you think the Alpha concept is treated so negatively and stereotyped as dark, mysterious, twisted, or evil? It's because the stereotype states that an Alpha is the epitome of this macho douche you always see in the movies picking on the little guy or the mean girl cheerleaders pushing down the nerdy girl in the library. That's not Alpha; that's just lame.

An Alpha is filled with compassion for those around them because they know that if someone in the group isn't doing well then it affects the rest, whether by way of morale or productivity. People can't follow someone unless you show them that even though you're better than them at certain things it doesn't mean you're above humanity; it means you have a responsibility to humanity, just like everyone else does.

Being an Alpha means holding a special position of trust, leadership, and guidance for those who need someone to look up to or to lead the way. An Alpha is not meant to be worshiped as a god, instead, you show compassion by being there for those that need you in every situation showing them that you're stronger together than apart, and always standing up for those who can't defend themselves.

You don't need to change who you are or how you were brought up to be an Alpha; it's really about changing the way you handle things because if your interactions with others are negative then people will see that as a reflection of yourself and not accept leadership. An Alpha is no better or worse than anyone else, but they do have more responsibility than most. It's time we stop vilifying the people that take on these responsibilities and start seeing their importance instead. Without real leaders that understand their own humanity and are willing to work to help humanity in their own communities, you end up with weak leaders who can be bought only looking out for their own best interests.

If we're ever going to advance humanity as a whole then every person needs to at least fill the void left by those before them regardless of whether they are an Alpha or not. We can no longer be okay with having our parents, mentors, friends, and idols leave behind someone worse than they are or who can't do the job as well. We need to be willing to step up and take on that responsibility for ourselves, each other, and our communities because there's no better time than now to change how we look at Alphas.

The forgotten Alpha

The True Alphas are our Mothers and Fathers, blood or not, that were always there no matter the cost to themselves. The Police, Firefighters, and other first responders running into danger to save others when everyone else runs away. The government officials working tirelessly to help the members of their community while others in their line of work take countless vacations and waste taxpayer money. Doctors and other medical professionals that work to cure the patient not just slap a patch on a gaping wound while prescribing medications that most likely won't work but come with a hefty payday for them. They are those that go above and beyond, understanding that their role is to be stronger than the rest so the rest can go on to become stronger than they thought they could.

The true meaning of being an Alpha has been long forgotten and pushed into the realm of fantasy or myth by weak individuals that want to exalt themselves as more than they are. Those who pretend to be a leader while only being manipulative narcissistic sycophants who love to hear themselves talk but rarely ever get anything of real value done. In all my years on this earth, more than half of which have been spent working side by side with real leaders, I've never seen an Alpha that was like that.

We need to bring back the real meaning behind being an Alpha and start working together as a society or we may as well just give up right now because it's going nowhere fast. We are woefully unprepared for anything resembling true chaos due to not only our lack of leadership but the incessant need by many to paint a demon on the face of anyone that resembles a leader so they can continue walking around terrorizing everyone with their bad behavior. None of them understands how bad it can really get out there. When you constantly appease the fire because you don't want to infringe on its perceived right to burn the forest you end up with scorched earth and nothing to show for it. The only problem is that this fire doesn't burn itself out, it just looks for something new to burn.

What will you do when everything goes dark for a week or two; no power, water, food deliveries? Nothing until someone finally takes charge long enough to get things moving again. The Alpha is always ready and willing to take on that responsibility either in their own social circle or in their community as a leader on a much larger scale. They do this whether they want to or not because it needs to be done. It isn't out of the need for glory, it is out of necessity alone.

To be an Alpha is to be willing to step up when no one else will. It's not about being a better person, it's about seeing what others refuse or are unwilling to see and doing something about it. People have become so jaded by the lies they tell themselves and everyone around them that they believe in those lies more than anything else. They would call someone like that crazy but I don't think they're any crazier than anyone else just because of how well they can handle what others can't. In fact, I find them saner than most; able to do what needs to be done directly instead of trying to convince you that an action is necessary when really their intentions were never pure from the beginning.

So let us take this time right now as we hurtle towards the end of this year and remember what it means to be an Alpha. Not the silly fantasy version but the real-world version that is willing to sacrifice themselves for those around them without a second thought; after all, that's exactly what they are doing when they do their job right. Never forget that we need them in more places than just our homes or workplaces. We need Heroes now more than ever before so let us start supporting each other and these amazing people wherever and whenever we can.

    Let us work together to build a stronger future

for those who come after us because we're the only ones that can do it. If you feel like an Alpha but don't know what this means or what I mean by this then I urge you to look around with fresh eyes and see if anyone out there deserves your help; stand up to the fire while everyone else cowers in its presence. Take charge even when no one thinks you're capable of doing so, trust me when I say there is someone out there right now that needs this from you more than anything else.

    To all the Alphas out there reading this, thank you for making our lives better by being in it no matter how big or small your actions may seem to others. You have no idea how much you mean to us, I hope you know that.

An Alpha Perseveres

What is perseverance?

Perseverance is the iron will to face a task and continue toward success no matter the odds that are stacked against you. It is the ability to keep trying despite repeated failure.

Perseverance, in short, means never giving up.

Perseverance is common among all Alphas. An Alpha knows that it's a dog-eat-dog world out there - you must be strong if you want to reap your rewards. It's not about how much power, money, and resources you have (though this helps) - it's all about how much dedication and hard work you can put into anything you do or set your mind to accomplish.

In many ways, perseverance is like the law of motion: objects in motion tend to stay in motion unless acted upon by an unbalanced force. In perseverance, this translates into persistence overcomes obstacles. If something is blocking your path then either find a way around it or break it down.

The difference between the average person and an Alpha is that Alphas realize even when they find a way around or break down an obstacle, there will almost always be another obstacle in its place. It's just a matter of time before one comes up - it's the nature of life. If you're determined enough to get through this new obstacle then you'll move on and never stop until you accomplish your goal.

But if the obstacles grow too much for you to handle by yourself then ask for help from others who have been where you are now and have made it. The only person who can ensure your success is YOU! Stand up again after every fall; refuse to stay beaten! Don't let other people's opinions cloud your judgment

Always finish what you start.

This doesn't mean to follow a course of action despite everything you might learn along the way. What it means is you must always see an action or task to its end, even if its end is finding out you were heading in the wrong direction, to begin with. Never be afraid to admit when you're wrong but always take accountability and the responsibility of correcting the course. Don't let minor failures or setbacks cause you to quit. Just move on and do it better next time.

Who knows, maybe that first try was the practice to get you ready for the final attempt? This is all about learning from your mistakes so take advantage of them. Every time you fail it's a chance to go back and do something better.

What separates winners from losers is the ability to recover quickly after falling down. A loser may lie there for days until somebody else kicks them off their pity pot; an Alpha will get right back up as soon as they hit the ground and come at you with more determination than ever before. Alphas never quit when things are tough because they realize it doesn't matter how much they're hurting, struggling, or exhausted because if they just keep going hard enough then eventually their hard work will pay off.

Don't let your ego get the best of you. This can be one of the hardest lessons to learn, especially as an Alpha - but it's a lesson many must learn if they want to succeed in life. Anytime something happens that makes you feel embarrassed or ashamed, just move on and don't look back with pride or defiance because it won't help you grow as a person nor will it make the situation any better. Just become more determined to do better next time! Never justify your mistakes by trying to argue what happened wasn't your fault because this brings no excuse for not performing well enough nor does it change anything that already happened. Simply accept what happened and move on. It's the only way to make progress in life.

Mistakes are inevitable, but you cannot let them hold you back! If anything, accept your mistakes as lessons that will help you grow into a stronger person. Everybody makes mistakes; it's how you deal with them is that sets apart winners from losers. Winners understand their mistakes were not due to a lack of effort or determination, nor do they excuse the situation by saying things like: "At least I tried my best" or "I couldn't have done any better." Instead, they realize that no matter what happens, it's never acceptable for them to quit at the first sign of trouble because their efforts aren't always going to be enough every time. A loser's mistake is an Alpha's learning experience and they never again make the same mistake twice!

Be honest with yourself about what you can and cannot do. For example, if you have little to no experience in playing guitar expect it to take a while for you to feel good enough at it to become self-confident - don't pretend it will only take a few days because then eventually when things are not progressing as quickly as expected you'll quit altogether out of frustration. However, if you go into the situation knowing that mastering this guitar skill may take months or years than just accept the work needed before expecting success.

Don't let the fear of making a mistake dictate your life. Mistakes are just that - mistakes - they don't define who you are as a person nor do they mean you're incapable of success. It's not about how many mistakes we make, but rather it's about how we deal with them and learn from them that determines our character. Winners are normally not afraid to try new things even if they think they may fail at it because disappointment is part of life and failure makes us stronger in time. Failure strengthens us by helping teach us valuable lessons such as what doesn't work or what we need to improve on for next time; which is all part of gaining the experience needed to become better. These lessons learned help create strong people capable of reaching their goals in the future.

If you're going to fail, do so while trying to succeed. Understand when things aren't working out and make a conscious decision that this isn't for you before giving up. But don't allow yourself to get sucked into feeling sorry for yourself or beginning to hate life because of one setback; it's a waste of time and only makes obstacles harder to deal with down the road. Instead, learn from your setbacks without getting discouraged and keep moving forward until you become successful at everything you try!

Being defeated is just another stepping stone on the path to victory – never quit until you have no other options! No matter what happens in life, always remain positive and throw your entire heart into all that you do because when you give it your all, at least you know that's what you can do. It is only after we have exhausted our efforts in every way possible that gives us the right to call ourselves defeated. This should never be an excuse to quit but rather, a reason for being proud of how hard we worked and learned through this process.

Keep moving forward no matter how difficult the task ahead may seem because nothing ever worthwhile comes easy! There are always going to be challenges thrown in our paths, the real question is are you willing to accept them as stepping stones to something great or will they end up breaking your stride? Allow yourself to get knocked down so many times by trying and failing – eventually, success will come! If things aren't working out for you, that's perfectly fine – all it means is that your plan isn't quite ready to be put into action yet, but with persistence and understanding your chances will grow.

Never lose faith.

Faith is something that comes from within. It is knowing deep within your soul that despite everything we may encounter it will all turn out alright if we just keep trying and moving forward.

A true Alpha never gives up no matter how hard the situation gets! They understand that some situations are going to be more challenging than others, but they don't allow themselves to give up – even when things look bad or feel impossible. Instead of quitting, Alphas just work harder by trying new ways of doing something until finally, an opportunity presents itself making it possible for them to get what they want. This same attitude transfers from their professional life into their personal lives too!

To be an Alpha is to constantly go against the odds and succeed in spite of them. It's knowing that no matter what obstacles are thrown at you if you continue working hard enough they will eventually begin to fall away making it possible for you to achieve your goals. Don't let anything or anyone tell you otherwise – nothing is impossible! If something looks like a challenge, never back down from it until you have tried every which way possible. This isn't about whether or not we succeed but rather how much effort we put into trying that makes all the difference.

When things seem darkest keep moving forward until you find the light.

There are always going to be times when life feels as though it's offering nothing but challenges and obstacles in our path; chances are these situations won't last forever. Sure, some of them may feel as though they're never going away but that doesn't mean we have to accept it as the truth or give up! If we are willing to keep moving forward with an open mind and a positive attitude new opportunities will eventually present themselves opening up doors for us to achieve greatness.

Life is full of ups and downs – don't let anything stop you from reaching your goals!

Perseverance is one of the most important qualities someone can possess. Even when things seem impossible or we feel like giving up, true Alphas continue fighting no matter what stands in their way because they understand what's worth fighting for and where they want to be in life. Life isn't about making excuses or explaining why something isn't possible - it's about being determined to not give up and finding new ways of getting what we want.

Success comes only after we've tried everything within our power to make something happen. Success isn't based on the results we receive but rather on how hard we work in order to get there. When life throws us a curveball, it will always be up to us whether or not we decide to strike out or stay at bat till the end. Despite difficult times and challenges, nothing is impossible as long as you are willing to push yourself beyond your limits; which often means having no one else around you who believes in your abilities more than you do!

We fail only when we stop trying and begin making excuses.

Alphas do not use excuses as an easy way to avoid responsibility for their actions – instead, they stand by them and try harder. When you make a mistake, don't allow yourself to hide from it. Admit what happened, learn your lesson from it and then move forward. Remember that making mistakes is often times the best opportunity for us to grow! If we aren't willing to accept this there's hardly any chance of improvement in our lives because we're always going to be looking at the past rather than working towards a bright future.

So remember: failure is impossible if you won't let it be the end! All it takes is hard work and determination – if something doesn't quite turn out the way you want it to, shake off the dust and keep pressing forward. The more you fail, the more your skills improve for future opportunities in life!

Be bold enough to change your approach when it doesn't work out and wise enough not to dwell on your failures. Life is full of ups and downs – never let anything get you down or stop you from achieving greatness because we deserve so much better than that. Be a fighter! Keep going until finally, our goals begin to become reachable no matter how far away they may seem at first. Being an Alpha is all about perseverance; having the guts to constantly go against the odds and do what's needed even if everything around us tells us it won't work out!

Once we've learned this trait we have truly achieved greatness within ourselves – being an Alpha isn't easy but perseverance will make the challenges worth it in the end. No matter how small or big they are, obstacles in our lives will always have the possibility of bringing us down but we choose how to deal with them. Once we stop allowing life's challenges to knock us around and instead start using them as stepping stones towards greatness; we'll never look back and regret not knowing what could've been possible if only we refused to give up!

The only thing which can truly stop us from achieving our goals is ourselves – don't let this happen! Think positive, keep pushing forward, and in no time you'll begin reaching your highest potentials in life. Life is already hard enough without having it beat you down further – stand up tall like a true Alpha!

Even in failure, we find success and only you can stop you!

Conclusion

Not everyone can be an Alpha but everyone needs one in their life.

The weak-minded in society with their victim complexes and their pseudoscientific descriptions of things filled with half-truths and even fewer facts are always going to be there to try to tear down everything good in this world. They believe they should be allowed to do what they want when they want and damn the consequences. They don't believe that you're rights or my rights matter if they in any way get in the way of their desires. The social justice warriors and mindless protestors of the world will flock toward any cause no matter the validity of the claim because dodos of a feather flock together.

There are real causes and real problems that we should all be facing together. However, when the current leaders in charge have no clue what they're doing and no intentions of really fixing the important issues, they make up issues for the weak-minded among us to fixate on so they won't pay attention to the real blunders happening all around them.

It saddens me when I see people that I have been close to all of my life falling for this garbage like it's a real problem, losing sight of everything else like they weren't aware of it a year earlier. How fast people's minds can be manipulated and changed with the correct prodding of emotions or a mixture of words. How the brain can be turned off and made to think that it's being stimulated when in reality they're just following a crowd without any real thoughts to them.

Is it the case that people are seeing something but not really seeing it?

Well, either way, you're no longer considered an individual but a number in one of the masses, and an Alpha has never for just being a number or a sheep in the herd.

Anyone that wishes to be considered an

Alpha in the truest sense doesn't need a group or other people to verify this. They are their own authority and know who they really are. They have had enough self-discipline, self-accountability, responsibility, and respect for themselves and others to see things for what they are without being tricked by social convention or peer pressure. They are successful at making the best out of everything in their lives, not just the bad. They use every opportunity available to be better than when they started and don't stop until they have achieved this goal. They self-actualize themselves; constantly evolving, improving, and never staying stagnant on any one thing for too long.

They're always grabbing new knowledge from a variety of sources and applying it to their own life's journey. Sometimes doing this even puts them ahead of others that believe they've already learned or that they know all there is to know about something because they heard someone else say it was true once but never questioned if it really was or not. Not everyone can be right all the time so why believe everything you hear? If you heard something once and it was a lie then the odds of it being true the second time are slim.

Sometimes this leads to someone trying to correct them on things they really don't even understand because they're still learning themselves. Then you get into arguments like, "Well I heard this," or "No that's what so-and-so said," or "I know but..." That's when you can tell the difference between an Alpha and everyone else. You can never serve two masters and an Alpha has none but themselves. If your mentality is that of a slave to the system then you can never see the light beyond the cloud they put in front of you.

Being an Alpha is having the courage to stand for what you truly believe in and to follow your own principles no matter how unpopular they may be. True Alphas don't let other people's opinions or beliefs limit them from acting on their true nature. They aren't influenced by the social norms of society that suppress others because that doesn't mean anything if it isn't based on the real truth. Truth is not a majority vote; the truth is just simply the way things really are.

People think they can hide behind a computer screen but all these keyboard warriors forget that actions speak louder than words, especially when you don't have any real-life accomplishments to back up those words with. My advice for anyone that's caught up in the lies of this world is to ask yourself, "Where do I really belong and what path am I truly on?" Are you an individual that has chosen their own way or are you a slave to the crowd?

An Alpha leads the pack because the pack needs the Alpha. The Alpha needs the pack but to a lesser yet significant degree. Without the Alpha, the pack falls apart or falls upon itself depending on the mentality of the pack. Without the pack, the Alpha just moves on because they know that eventually, a new pack will come along. There's always someone looking for a leader.

This doesn't mean you need to be a manipulative narcissistic prick to be an Alpha; it's actually the contrary. You need to be compassionate to those around you but confident enough to give them a kick in the ass when necessary. You also need to understand when the crowd's opinion doesn't benefit you or them and be willing to strike out on your own.

To be an Alpha means having a rare strength within that you don't find in many people these days. An Alpha is someone that everyone needs in their lives whether they understand it or not. You can't force them to see the light, some never will because it is their path to walk and their lessons to learn. An Alpha is meant to be better; not to wave it in the face of everyone behind them, but to serve as an example so that when the right pack comes along they will follow and become better themselves.

    Be an Alpha so that the right pack may follow and know the way. Let the universe sort out the rest.

www.ingramcontent.com/pod-product-compliance
Lightning Source LLC
Chambersburg PA
CBHW071450220526
45472CB00003B/750